Kn
the
Upanishads

Ramanuj Prasad

PUSTAK MAHAL®

Publishers
Pustak Mahal®

J-3/16 , Daryaganj, New Delhi-110002
☎ 23276539, 23272783, 23272784 • *Fax:* 011-23260518
E-mail: info@pustakmahal.com • *Website:* www.pustakmahal.com

Sales Centre
- 10-B, Netaji Subhash Marg, Daryaganj, New Delhi-110002
  ☎ 23268292, 23268293, 23279900 • *Fax:* 011-23280567
  E-mail: rapidexdelhi@indiatimes.com
- Hind Pustak Bhawan
  6686, Khari Baoli, Delhi-110006
  ☎ 23944314, 23911979

Branches
Bengaluru: ☎ 080-22234025 • *Telefax:* 080-22240209
E-mail: pustak@airtelmail.in • pustak@sancharnet.in
Mumbai: ☎ 022-22010941, 022-22053387
E-mail: rapidex@bom5.vsnl.net.in
Patna: ☎ 0612-3294193 • *Telefax:* 0612-2302719
E-mail: rapidexptn@rediffmail.com
Hyderabad: *Telefax:* 040-24737290
E-mail: pustakmahalhyd@yahoo.co.in

© **Pustak Mahal, New Delhi**

ISBN 978-81-223-0831-1

Edition: 2010

Printed at : Param Offsetters, Okhla, Delhi-110020

Dedication

*Dedicated to the service of
my teacher of Vedānta
H.H. Swāmi Paramārtānanda
196/A, St. Mary's Road,
Abhramapuram,
Chennai.*

Contents

Foreword

The Upanishads are the very quintessence of Indian wisdom, the blossoms of the finest thoughts gleaned from the dialectical relationship of wisdom teachers and their diligent students – the *Guru shishya parasparyam*.

Though the Upanishadic lore has been known in India for centuries, it is only in recent times that the teachings came to be known to the non-Sanskrit-speaking world. One of the earliest translations of the Upanishads was into Persian with the assistance of pandits from Benares at the behest of Prince Dara Shikoh in 1657. The Persian version was subsequently translated into the Latin *Oupnek'hat* by Anquetil Duperron in 1802. The teachings of the Upanishads became known in Europe through the German translation done by Franz Mischel in 1882.

Today we live in an unprecedented age where knowledge has overcome all past boundaries. More people are educated now than ever before. But the complexities of life along with deep anxiety and uncertainty have vitiated the joy and new-found freedom. It is as if mankind is navigating through uncharted waters. These circumstances make the teachings of the Upanishads very relevant and valuable to reorient our lives in a correct manner with a proper structure of values.

The teachings of the Upanishads clearly state the goal and purpose of life. They promise deliverance from ignorance and the associated pain and suffering. Unalloyed happiness is gained by the proper understanding of one's own true nature, as well as that of the world in which we live. The philosophy of Vedānta, which is based on the teachings of the Upanishads, begins with two questions: *Ko aham?* (Who am I?) and *Kuto jagat?* (Whence this world?). The teachings of the Upanishads give an enduring and convincing answer to these fundamental questions and bestow great peace of mind.

We are fortunate that in the author, Ramanuj Prasad, we have a well-disciplined academic mind along with mature understanding and original thinking. He has competently and systematically explained the teachings of the Upanishads by taking one of the finest, the *Mundaka*, as his theme. He has also given apt references from other major Upanishads like the *Brihadāranyaka*, *Kena*, *Svetāsvatara* and *Katha* to show the underlying unity of *Brahma Vidyā*, or the Science of the Absolute. The *Mundaka Upanishad* has evolved from the *Atharva Veda*, which is also the source of other highly mystical Upanishads like the *Prasna*. In the *Mundaka Upanishad* Guru Angiras instructs the ascetic Shaunaka on *"that knowledge on knowing which nothing remains to be known"*.

With this highest of teachings as his subject, Ramanuj Prasad has kept the common reader in mind. For centuries, the Upanishadic treasure of wisdom has been confined to very few people. With its clear logical presentation, this book will render sterling service in spreading the sublime teachings of the Upanishads to all readers. The aspirant seeking wisdom as well as the scholarly person keen to deepen his or her understanding of the Upanishads will benefit from this book.

H.H. Swãmi Vyãsa Prasãd
Nãrãyana Gurukula,
Fernhill – 643004,
Tamil Nadu.

Invocation

This is a prayer to the Lord for successful completion of a work undertaken and the work is offered to the Lord as service to Him. Therefore, whatever may be the credit that accrues, even in the future, it belongs to the Lord. The individual being an instrument in the hands of the Lord, one remains only an agent for name's sake; the actual work is done by Him and for Him.

In our tradition, all work is undertaken only after invoking the Lord's blessings. The very creator of the Universe Brahman also began the work of creation of the Universe after uttering the words *OM TAT SAT* (the triple designation of Brahman), which is the very essence of the essence. This is said to be the reason that creation is so perfect and flawless. The invocation stands on the same plane as that of a *shãnti pãtha* of the spiritual works. It is also a norm that we should not study any spiritual work that does not have the Lord's name or a prayer at the start. Auspiciousness is indicated through the invocation and without that, it is neither auspicious nor a fruitful work.

Thus, invocation of the blessings of the Lord for the work is through a prayer to Lord Krishna, who is the teacher of all teachers of spirituality, which is the very goal of human life. Lord Krishna is the son of the Universal Mother Devaki, incarnated in the family of Vasudeva from the Vrishnis dynasty. Lord Krishna is the destroyer of Kansa and Chānoora, the enemies of virtuous thoughts and deeds.

The verse:

वसुदेवसुतं देवं कंसचाणूरमर्दनम्
देवकीपरमानन्दं कृष्णं वन्दे जगद्गुरुम ।

I salute Lord Krishna, the world teacher, the son of Vasudeva and the supreme bliss of Devaki, the destroyer of Kansa and Chānoorā.

This is one of the verses in the *Gita dhyanam* and is chanted before the study of the same. As discussed later in the example of the Upanishad, normally *shānti pātha* is from that Veda to which that particular Upanishad belongs. Similarly, here it should have been from the *Mahābhārata* of which the *Bhagavad Gītā* is a part. But in this case it is not so, as the invocation was incorporated by the recent āchārya, Madhusudhana Saraswati, for the study of the *Bhagavad Gītā*.

Hari Om!

□□□

Introduction

There is a verse signifying that most of the functional instincts between human beings and animals are common — such as hunger, thirst, fear and procreation. What is exclusive to humans is the power of thought. Human beings can think clearly, analyse a situation objectively and take appropriate measures for a better future, whereas animals have no faculty to think and choose. Their behaviour is programmed and no improvement is possible under the laws of nature.

If one interviews people at the New Delhi Railway Station or the inter-state bus terminus and asks what made them come there at that point of time, there will be as many answers as the individuals questioned. One may say he is going to the office, another to the Parliament session, the third to meet the President or to visit the RTO office, hospital, school, library, Rājghāt and so on and so forth. It will appear that there are innumerable objectives being pursued by human beings. But if little more thought is given to these multifarious activities, one can see that all lead to one common goal : the perennial search for happiness.

Without any doubt, all activities are means to happiness and may not be pursued if they resulted in pain or discomfort. This is true even in the case of one's wife, husband, son, daughter and a host of other relatives and related objects who or which are all means only. The lineage of the family, one proudly claims to belong to, is also a means to happiness only. The objectives enumerated so far are external to one, come to join at a point of time and similarly leave too. Therefore, whatever happiness we get out of them is dependent on the source, which is not the inner part of the self as heat in the fire but like the heat of the water.

The happiness that comes from external objects is borrowed. The only internal happiness is the independent one, which is the very nature of human beings. Happiness that comes from external objects will certainly vanish and this threat always exists. The external sources of happiness are governed by many conditions that have to be fulfilled for enjoying happiness. One has to work hard to fulfil them in order to be happy occasionally. Whenever the conditions are not fulfilled, they leave a trail of pain proportionate to the happiness one got out of it. In fact, there is no pleasure from external sources but simply a rearrangement of the problem, much like the relief felt after shifting a load from one shoulder to the other.

With concern, compassion and love equal to that of thousands of mothers, the Veda (Scriptures) promises assistance for both types of happiness – that born out of external objects or that which is the intrinsic nature of every human being. The choice is left to the individual. The Veda never forces anyone to choose either, but cautions that all pleasures dependent on anything are temporary, unreal and also a source of pain in equal measure.

The first portion of the Veda contains rituals to attain worldly happiness and is capable of fulfilling whatever desire one has, be it for a son, wealth, wife, fame, complexion, etc, all of which can be attained through *karma* and rituals. However, the end part of the Veda insists on renunciation of all worldly possessions and desires – the 'less luggage, more comfort' principle. Its concern is in the discovery of the 'Self', just like the lost prince who was not aware of the fact that he was a prince and had to be told: "You are a prince of this kingdom; arise to *claim* your own glory."

This is the wisdom of the Upanishads that we will study objectively in the subsequent pages, as the reward for this knowledge far surpasses the acquisition of the entire world's wealth. Such happiness lies in completeness, which external objects can never give one to feel complete, as they are all ephemeral in nature. Knowledge of the Upanishads is liberation ; it leads to internal happiness, which is one's own nature.

A quotation conveys the fact that happiness is the very embodiment of a spiritual peak:

"(He) knew Bliss as Brahman; for from Bliss, indeed, all these beings originate; having been born, they are sustained by Bliss; they move towards and merge in Bliss. This knowledge realised by Bhrigu and imparted by Varuna (starts from the food-self and) terminates in the Supreme (Bliss), established in the cavity of the

heart. He who knows this becomes firmly established; he becomes the possessor of food and the eater of food; and he becomes great in progeny, cattle and the lustre of holiness, and great in glory."

–Taittiriya Upanishad (III, V-1)

The Upanishads are the basic foundation and the fountainhead of philosophical wisdom, the eternal truth and the religion of mankind. No other literature of the world can match the thoughts that are taught in the Upanishads and were accepted as the ultimate by the greatest thinkers of the time such as Sanatkumāra, Yājnavalkya and Shankara. While the language of the Upanishads is rich in grandeur and sublimity, its simplicity and spiritual beauty also cannot be missed.

The idea and the concept that is very difficult even to imagine has been so successfully infused into one's mind that the student is hijacked from the lower self to the higher self, even before one can realise that one is not the old self. At times one is lifted to that height of poetic grandeur from where the finest music of the relative world remains only an irritating noise. Time has not been able to diminish the lustre of the Upanishads, as they remain ever fresh, sustaining their beauty as though they had just captured the fragrance of the flowers, the energy of the morning sun and the beauty of the full moon in winter.

The Upanishads take one by the hand to the other shore where immortality is waiting with a garland in its open arms. And the hand is gripped lest one may not fall back. Therefore, let that lead one so that one may not free the hand, as the guide is trustworthy and sincere to your cause alone.

This introductory volume focuses on the essentials of the Upanishads, along with a brief illustration of the content in the *Mundakopanishad*. A few parallel mantras are drawn from the other Upanishads, as an exercise to appreciate the universal nature of the facts in Upanishadic teachings, since they belong to the Vedas, which is universal by implication.

Basic Upanishads

Amongst the Upanishads, there are many minor Upanishads dealing only with one or the other aspects of the principal Upanishads. Adi Shankaracharya and other acharyas have commented upon the ten principal Upanishads too.

These ten Upanishads are known by various names, such as 'Fundamental Upanishads', 'Old Upanishads', 'Genuine Upanishads' and so on, but whatever their name, these ten Upanishads are the very essence of the Vedanta philosophy contained in the Vedas.

1. Ishãvãsya Upanishad: This is also known as *Vajasaneyi Upanishad* and has beautifully brought out the path of renunciation for *sannyãsis* and for others with an active life-style who are not yet ready for *sannyãsa* but want to worship *Hiranyagarbha* together with the unborn *prakriti*. Esoteric terms such as *vidyã*, *avidyã*, *sambhuti* and the like have been used at various points, which make the Upanishads not easily understandable, though apparently simple. The very first line of the first mantra is a very popular quotation *Ishāvāsyamidam Sarvam*, "This whole world is covered by the Lord", which induces a thrilling inspiration in the mind of the student.

2. Kena or Talavakra Upanishad: *Kena* (by whom) has the essentials for comprehension of Brahman, who is behind all the instruments of knowledge, such as eye of the eyes, ear of the ears etc, and learning under the guidance of a preceptor has been emphasised. Liberation cannot be attained by karma or knowledge combined with karma. Knowledge of Ātman is antagonistic to karma and cannot, therefore, co-exist.

Karmas are to be performed without expectation of fruits to purify the mind and to gain strong desire for the final emancipation. Karma alone cannot ensure immortality. The nature of Brahman is also dealt with, as Brahman is beyond the reach of the senses and the mind.

3. Kathopanishad: The most beautiful Upanishad that answers questions like "What happens when one dies? Is everything gone with death or does something survive? What is that beyond dharma and adharma, knowledge and ignorance and birth and death etc?" It is verily the Supreme Lord.

These and many other topics have been answered in a very natural manner for an easy under-standing, through a dialogue between Lord Yama, the teacher and Nachiketā, a serious, honest and motivated student who has an understanding of the eternal and the ephemeral in full measure. He is a young boy of about 12 years, the son of Vajasravā, who once said in anger: "I will give you to death."

The boy is very devoted to his father and society and has a strong desire for Self knowledge, which is the greatest of benefits one can imagine. When Lord Yama agreed to grant him three boons, the lad asked for (a) pacification of his father (b) a fire ritual to gain heaven and (c) knowledge of the Self.

This Upanishad is very popular not only in India but also abroad. In the elevation of thoughts, depth of expressions, and the beauty of its imagery, no Upanishad is equal to the *Kathopanishad.*

4. Prashnopanishad: This Upanishad is a commentary on the *Mundakopanishad* and the mantras dealt with in the *Mundakopanishad* have been dealt with more elaborately here. Six seekers of Brahman go to the teacher Pippalāda and put six questions pertaining to cosmology, the *devas*, the nature and origin of *prāna*, sleep and dream, *Pranava* or *OM* and *Purusha* of sixteen *kalās* or parts. One uniform idea runs through the *Prashna, Mundaka* and *Māndukya Upanishads.*

5. Mundakopanishad: The word *Mundaka* applies to its division (chapter) and the ritual of carrying fire on the shaven head. Its verses are in mantra form (sacred verses) meant for *sannyāsis* (shaved head). This Upanishad makes a systematic approach to the topic of knowledge of the Self dispassionately through discrimination. The fitness of the student goes along with symbolic rituals presented before taking up the study. This ritual has significance to the disciplined body-mind complex.

6. Mandukyopanishad: *Manduka* means a frog. Lord Varuna assumes the form of a frog to reveal the significance and superiority of *OM* or *Pranava* or *OMKĀRA*, the only name and symbol of the Brahman. The importance of the name remains still alive though the person has gone, according to Rāma, Shankara and others. The text of the Upanishad declares that OM, Brahman and Ātman are all one and the same. OM is a word that stands for all sounds, words or names. The word *akshara* means "that which is imperishable or immortal", which is of the same nature as the higher *nirguna Brahman* – Brahman without attributes, as well as *saguna Brahman* – the lower Brahman, that is, Brahman with attributes.

7. Aitareya Upanishad: This Upanishad is attributed to Rishi Aitareya. It does not mean that this is his own philosophy, but simply that it was revealed to him by the Lord. It has three chapters.

Chapter I contains three sections dealing with *Shrishti Prakaranam* – creation of the world, to show ultimately as *mithyā*. The second chapter deals with various stages of *Jiva*, including its tenure in the womb of the mother. Ādi Shankarāchārya says this is to show the miseries, the Jiva has to undergo so that the *sādhaka* gets *vairāgyam* – total detachment. The third chapter deals fully only with Brahman, revealing the identity between the Jiva and Brahman. Out of the four important *mahāvākyas*, *prajnānam Brahman* – awareness – is nothing but Brahman; the *jagat kāranam* occurs in this Upanishad.

Just as in the *Kenopanishad*, this Upanishad also declares: "Who is he whom we meditate upon as Ãtman? That indeed is the Ãtman by which a living being sees form, hears sound, smells scent, articulates speech and discriminates between what is sweet and what is not. That which is the heart and the mind is the same as that. All are but names of *Prajñā* or *Consciousness*. The whole world is formed in *Prajñā* and, therefore, *Prajna* is Brahman."

8. Taittiriya Upanishad: This Upanishad is famous as it preserves the traditional recitation of the verses. Even today, it is often chanted during household rituals, though not necessarily in the proper context.

The words *Satyam jnanam anantam Brahman* declared in this Upanishad are a revelation of the relationship between the *Jiva, jagat* and *Ishwara* – the Infinite Lord. The *Shikshāvalli* chapter is famous for its teaching to students who are leaving for home after completing their studies. It teaches them values in life and how to conduct themselves in society and progress towards the goal of human birth.

This Upanishad has three parts under the titles *Shikshāvalli, Ānandavalli* and *Bhriguvalli*. The second part, Ānandavalli, deals exclusively with *Brahma vidyā*. It declares that "the Bliss perceivable on the perfection of desireless living is enjoyed by one who realises Brahman and that is the only real *Bliss*".

9. Chhāndogya Upanishad: The singer of *Sāma Veda* (Chhandas) is a Chhāndoga and the beliefs and practices are set forth in the *Chhāndogya Upanishad*.

The first five chapters of the Upanishad are about worship and meditation (duality). The Upanishad emphasises *udgita*, the recitation of OM as the means to purify the mind. It tells many stories in simple language to drive home the profound subject matter. The initial chapters advocate rituals and meditation for all material gains for ordinary people but also warns that they will not ensure liberation or immortality.

Chapter six is about Brahman and the famous statement *Tattvam asi* (*That thou art*) is from this Upanishad. This Upanishad sets our goal as 'Self knowledge' and not material pleasures and enjoyment.

10. Brihadāranyaka Upanishad: *Brihad* means 'big' or 'great' and *āranyaka* denotes 'forest', the knowledge that is taught in the forest, the *Brahma vidyā*. A ranking Upanishad, besides being the biggest Upanishad in size, the commentary, the substance, the theme, the voluminous subject matter and the explanation of Ãtman in the *Brihadāranyaka Upanishad* are all great.

There is hardly any point that cannot be found here. Many doctrines like *bheda-abheda*, *mimāmsa*, *visishtādvaita* etc (difference-cum-identity, analysis and qualified monism) have been discussed vis-à-vis the Vedānta. The *madhukhanda* and *yājnavalkyakhanda* are divisions giving many illumining illustrations of the Advaita doctrine and nature, *upadesha* and *upāsanā*. The presentation of *adhyaropa* and *apavada* is in full play to explain the real and unreal (*mithyā*) substance. Many logical explanations, such as *sambandha* and *vidyā-avidyā sutras* are seen displayed throughout the glory of Ādi Shankarāchārya.

The famous statement *Aham Brahmasmi* (I am Brahman) of the *Yajur Veda* is found here. The verses are obscure and it would have been impossible to study these without the commentary of Ādi Shankarāchārya.

Some important concepts:

➤ The infinite fullness (plenum) alone is bliss and there is no bliss in small finite things.

➤ The infinite fullness is immortal and the finite mortal.

➤ The infinite fullness is alone everywhere and it is all this.

➤ In purity of food there is purity of nature.

➤ Only the Self is dear and everything other than the Self comes and goes with time.

➤ The Self is the Absolute and those who know as much become indestructible.

➤ He who knows that God and he are different is a beast.

➤ By knowing the Self as everything, everything becomes known, just as gold is the content of all ornaments and clay is of all pots.

➤ Consciousness is Brahman and the world has Consciousness for its functioning. All this is Brahman – the ultimate reality, and knowing this is realisation. He who realises this becomes immortal.

➤ Brahman is the only reality and all other things are ephemeral (*mithya*), which includes all the gross and subtle, micro and macro worlds.

➤ Brahman is the intelligent and material cause of the world.

I convey my heartfelt thanks to Mr Ramamurthy for his assistance in preparing this work.

Hari Om!

–Ramanuj Prasad

❑❑❑

Shānti Pātha

This is a prayer recited by both the teacher and the student together, to ward off obstacles in the process of the study of the Scriptures as well as that of life, in preserving the faculties of the body of both the teacher and the student, so that the knowledge imparted is assimilated properly. The prayer is addressed to the *Adhishtāna Devatā* – the presiding deity of the total power of all the organs.

The hearing faculty is most required by the student and then, the faculty of sight; therefore, the first prayer is to that God. Subsequent prayers are addressed to the Lords of all energy so that, after the learning, it can be practised and propagated to the next generation. Body and limbs should be strong so that one can live up to the allotted duration of life and continue to hear and sing the glory of the Lord till the last breath.

The word *shānti* is chanted thrice to take cognisance of three types of obstacles that can come in the way of a practitioner (a *sādhaka*):

➤ Obstacles arising from one's own body-mind complex.

➤ Obstacles from the immediate surroundings.

➤ Obstacles from supernatural forces.

Obstacles from one's own body may be in the form of incapacity and loss of endurance of faculties to undertake the task of listening to the teachings, understanding clearly and assimilating their direct and indirect meanings. Immediate surrounding relates to the vicinity, the factors that are capable of hijacking the attention and interest in the study over which one has limited control. Supernatural powers are the divine dispensation over which one has absolutely no control at all, such as an earthquake, rain, storm or any other type of obstacle that can endanger the process and progress.

One may have doubts as to why one should pray to the Lord, as the Lord Himself can grace the individual with all protection, as He knows every thought and act of beings. While this is true, there are two points to be noted:

1. One should make the effort to create a positive thrust in the phenomenal world in one's own favour and also to cultivate the mental strength for forbearance.

2. The Lord wishes that one should expressively seek the grace, that is, the surrender of ego, and submit one's self to earn the grace. It is like conserving water even when it is raining heavily and harvesting the energy of heat when the sun is blazing. One should channelise the grace to one's advantage.

The *shãnti pãtha* that we have here belongs to the *Atharva Veda*. All the Upanishads from this Veda will have the same *shãnti pãtha*.

ॐ भद्रं कर्णेभिः शृणुयाम देवा भद्रं पश्येमाक्षभिर्यजत्राः ।
स्थिरैरङ्गैस्तुष्टुवाग्ँसस्तनूभिः व्यशेम देवहितं यदायुः ।
स्वस्ति न इन्द्रो वृद्धश्रवाः स्वस्ति नः पूषा विश्ववेदाः ।
स्वस्ति नस्ताक्ष्यों अरिष्टनेमिः स्वस्ति नो बृहस्पतिर्दधातु ।।
ॐ शान्तिः! शान्तिः!! शान्तिः!!!!

The first prayer is for bestowing blessings on the instruments of knowledge (*Jnānendriyas*). Here only two have been talked about (representative) but the prayer is for all Gods of the instruments of knowledge. It says, "Let our ears always hear auspicious sounds only and our eyes may be used to see only what is auspicious and good."

There is nothing more auspicious than the name of the Lord and his glorious creation present all the time. A true devotee of the Lord neither asks to leave early nor to stay longer than what is allotted. Therefore, here the prayer is to be fit in physical and mental health throughout the prescribed period, which is not for the sense pleasures of the world but to be fully dedicated in His service and praise. Lord Indra represents strength and the Lord of the Sun (*Surya Devatā*) grants nourishment and, therefore, they are addressed for the grant of strong limbs and nourishment that is required by the body-mind complex to be sustained in harmony.

The vehicle of swift motion without any obstruction from any quarter, *Garuda* is propitiated to grace unobstructed passage in all undertakings.

Hari Om!

❑❑❑

TOPIC – I
Upanishads Explained

The Meaning of *Upanishad*

The word *Upanishad* can be split as *upa-ni-shad*. The meaning of the split-up is as follows:

Upa – near go to the teacher of knowledge.

Ni – the destroyer.

Shad – of the *samsāra* (which indicates mortality, old age, disease etc. In a nutshell, it indicates the cycle of birth and death.).

To sum up: The science of granting freedom from the miseries of the world, the Upanishad must only be learnt from a competent teacher of the Scriptures.

Vedānta: As it is located generally at the end of all four Vedas, it is known as *Veda-anta* (*anta* = end). It is not the end but the conclusion of Vedas.

Jnāna Kānda: Division of topics in the Vedas is known as *Kānda* and that division which discusses the knowledge portion is known as *Jnāna Kānda* and by implication it indicates the Upanishad.

Brahman Vidyā: That knowledge which discusses the subject matter of the Absolute and its relationship with the individual and the Universe.

Ãtma Vidyã: The knowledge of the content of the manifest and unmanifest worlds (the world that exists in the seed form, just as the seed contains the tree, the branches and the leaves etc, and all definitions in potential form – not perceivable at this stage).

The Upanishads discuss the following six topics in general and one does not find any systematic approach, but this deficiency has been made good in the *Brahma Sutra* of Maharishi Vyasãchãrya.

➤ Who is *Jiva?*
➤ Who is *Ishwara?*
➤ What is *Jagat?*
➤ What is bondage?
➤ What is liberation?
➤ What are the means of liberation?

The Vedas contain many Upanishads that reveal the identity of *Jiva* with Brahman/ *Ishwara.* The earlier tally of the Upanishads was one hundred and eighty, but only one hundred and eight are now available. Of these, Ãdi Shankarãchãrya has commented upon ten Upanishads only. Known as the principal Upanishads, these are:

➤ *Ishavãsya Upanishad*
➤ *Kenopanishad*
➤ *Kathopanishad*
➤ *Prashnopanishad*
➤ *Mundakopanishad*
➤ *Mãndukya Upanishad*
➤ *Taittiriya Upanishad*

➤ *Aitareya Upanishad*

➤ *Chhāndogya Upanishad*

➤ *Brihadāranyaka Upanishad*

Kenopanishad and *Chhandogya Upanishad* belong to the *Sāma Veda*; *Mundakopanishad*, *Māndukya Upanishad* and *Prashnopanishad* belong to *Atharva Veda*; *Ishāvāsya Upanishad* and *Brihadāranyaka Upanishad* belong to *Shukla Yajurveda*; *Kathopanishad* and *Taittiriya Upanishad* belong to *Krishna Yajurveda* and *Aitareya Upanishad* belongs to *Rig Veda*. These are four Veda Samhitās – *Rig, Yajur, Sama* and *Atharva Veda*.

Rig Veda is in poetry form, *Yajur Veda* is in prose form, *Sāma Veda* contains Rig mantras in musical form. All the Upanishads uniformly declare : *Brahma satyam, jagan mithyā jivo brahmaiva na parah.*

"It is a *mahāvākya* wherein the relative world is described as unreal – its existence is dependent on Brahman (Ātmā), the real, independent existence and the substratum of the universe. The *Jiva* (individual) without equipments and *Ishwara* (without equipments) are renamed as Brahman and they are one and the same. (They are not two entities.)"

The reason for selecting only these ten Upanishads and not others by Ãdi Shankarāchārya is that Maharishi Vyāsāchārya has based his famous work *Brahma Sutra* mostly on these ten Upanishads. The available 108 Upanishads cover the subject matter of the earlier Upanishads in its entirety; similarly, these ten Upanishads cover all the essentials.

Without any loss of ideas, these ten Upanishads can also be compressed into five: the *Mundaka, Māndukya, Taittiriya, Katho* and *Kenopanishad.* Of these five, the *Kathopanishad* and *Mundakopanishad* highlight all aspects of Vedānta. Between these two, the *Mundakopanishad* is the smaller one, containing about sixty verses, against one hundred and twenty of *Kathopanishad.* Therefore, here we deal with the *Mundakopanishad* in greater detail.

Hari Om!

❑❑❑

TOPIC – II
Whom the Upanishad Addresses

The Upanishad undertakes the responsibility of spiritual welfare of each individual, who in turn serves, as per tradition, groups that form the society and the nation. Through this approach, Vivekānanda, Sri Rāmakrishna and Ramana Maharishi made a tremendous impact on the masses of their time and even today, decades after leaving their mortal body, there are deep imprints that perpetuate their teachings without any boundary.

Similarly, the Upanishads are a source of strength to mankind as it reveals that the children of the Omnipotent and Omniscient all-powerful God are not meek and weak creatures but have inherited the very nature of the Lord.

The Upanishad addresses them as immortal and all-powerful ones. It reminds them: "You are not a lamb but a lion and so, come and discover yourself. You do not have to lean on anyone and, in fact, the whole universe is leaning on your support – the support of all is Self-supported." –

In the hour of relative uncertainty and distress, the Upanishad stands with us and inspires us to rise to the occasion with confidence and strength. It convinces us to demonstrate that one can live and help others to live without over-anxiety about the past and the future. The knowledge of the Upanishad presupposes the knowledge given by the Upanishad. The Upanishad is an instrument of knowledge and not conversion of knowledge at a later date. It imparts knowledge of the Absolute. It uses ingenious methods and peculiar language to convey that knowledge which is beyond description and comparison.

Also, the words have more than one meaning at times and, therefore, it becomes necessary to ascertain that particular meaning in the given context of the subject matter. So the import of the idea demands correct interpretation of the Veda of which the Upanishad happens to be a part and parcel. Though, the Upanishad forms a part of the Veda, it differs sharply as the pursuits are different, the benefits derived are different and the method of study too is different.

Thus, the Upanishad aims at knocking out the duality by arriving at *mahāvākyas* – statement of facts on the unity of *Jiva* and *Ishwara*. There are many ingenious techniques to prove the identity of *Jiva* with *Ishwara*. This assertion is combined with differentiation between the real and the unreal spirit and matter etc.

Some of the techniques are:

➤ Discrimination through the five sheaths (*Pancha kosha viveka*) known as *annamaya, prānamaya, manomaya, vijnānamaya* and *ānandamaya koshas.*

➤ Three-body analysis (*sharira trayam*) – gross, subtle and causal bodies.

➤ Three states of existence (*avastha trayam*) – waking, dream and dreamless sleep.

➤ Subject-object division (*driga-drishya-viveka*) – seer and seen analysis.

Mahāvākyas are expressions of ascertaining the identity of the *Jiva* with Brahman. The Upanishads have many such expressions but four of them are given as representative from each Veda:

➤ **Prajnānam Brahman:** (प्रज्ञानं ब्रह्म) – Perception, direction, understanding, knowledge, retentive power, vision, firmness, power of reflection, freedom of thinking, mental depression, memory, recollection, determination, vitality, desire, love – all these are but names of *Prjnāna* or Consciousness. This is Brahman. (*Aitareya Upanishad-3.1 – Rig Veda*).

➤ **Tat tvam asi:** (तत्त्वमसि) – That which is the subtlest of all is the Self of all this. It is the truth. It is the Self. That thou art. (*Chhāndogya Upanishad VI-VIII-7 – Sāma Veda*).

➤ **Aham Brahmāsmi:** (अहं ब्रह्मास्मि) – The sage Vamadeva, while realising this (Self) as 'That' knew, 'I was Manu, and the sun.' And to this day, whoever in like manner knows It as "I am Brahman" becomes all this (universe). (*Brihadaranyaka Upanishad I-IV-10 – Yajur Veda*).

➤ **Ayam Ātmā Brahman :** (अयमात्मा ब्रह्म) – All this is Brahman. This Ātmā (the Supreme Self) is Brahman. (*Māndukya Upanishad 2 – Atharva Veda*).

33

In order to assimilate these *mahāvākyas* and to bring them into the reality of understanding despite day-to-day transactions, this will continue to be different, just as we have the understanding that the sun does not actually rise, though in the relative plane, we do experience this. To know the Ātmā, the Self, one must resort to *Jnāna yoga*. *Jnāna yoga* is also known as *Brahma vidyā* or *adhyātma vidyā* and all mean the same – knowledge of the Self.

The threefold practices in this knowledge are:

➤ **Shravanam** – listening to the teachings of Vedānta through a guru.

➤ **Mananam** – clearing of doubts arising during the course of listening.

➤ **Nidhidhyāsanam** – getting rid of the habitual tendency of slipping back.

Listening (*shravanam*) involves faith in the teacher and in the Scriptures, understanding the meanings of the Upanishadic interpretation of words and sentences, asking questions to clarify doubts and retaining what has been taught and the relationship of what is being repeated as an emphasis and the essence of the teachings.

Analytical thinking (*mananam*) is reflected in the teachings to have an objective perception. For example, the word 'I' has a different meaning when it is used in the transactional world than what the word means in Vedānta or in the real sense. The attributes of the body-mind complex should be separated from the real 'I', which is attributeless and is neither the 'doer' nor an 'enjoyer'.

A thorough understanding of Ātma and *anātma* is known as contemplation (*nidhidhyāsanam*). This involves a mind that is alert even while conducting day-to-day worldly activities. One is likely to miss the point and see the functions of *anātma* on Atma due to die-hard habits, which have to be corrected continuously till we get out of the hold of old habits and our understanding becomes firm. We may compare this to the burning of the boat after reaching the shore.

While *shravanam* is associated with the help of the guru and the Scriptures, *mananam* may be done by oneself or with the help of the guru or a person on whom we have confidence, whereas *nidhidhyāsanam* is totally a self-effort.

In the words of the great sage Yajnavalkya:

आत्मा वा अरे द्रष्टव्यः श्रोतव्यो मन्तव्यो निदिध्यासितव्यो
मैत्रेह्यात्मनो वा अरे दर्शनेन श्रवणेन मत्या विज्ञानेनेदगं सर्वं विदितम् ।।

Maitreyi, the Self should be realised, should be heard of, reflected on and meditated upon. By the realisation of the Self through hearing, reflection and meditation, all this is known.

–Brihadāranyaka Upanishad 2.4.10

We have discussed the practice of knowledge of the Self, knowledge of the Ātmā, through *shravanam, mananam* and *nidhidhyāsanam*, but it is not so simple, otherwise there would not have been any glory in its attainment. The fact is that the Upanishad takes it for granted that all those who come for knowledge of the Self are prepared students. It is assumed that the student has undergone all the necessary disciplines and has been equipped with a disciplined mind and sense. This is also known as spiritual values (*daivi sampat*), gained through *karma, upāsanā* or *bhakti* or through such practices like austerity, charity, and rituals.

Known as *sādhanā chatushtaya sampati*, the outline of these qualifications is:

➤ Discriminative knowledge between the timeless (*nitya*) and the time-bound (*anitya*).

➤ Dispassion for the enjoyment of the objects that are the fruits (of actions) here (in this world) and there (in heaven).

➤ The sixfold disciplines of mind and sense control.

➤ Intense desire for liberation.

Now the sixfold wealth is detailed here as *sāmah, damah, uparamah, titikashā, shraddhā* and *samādhānam*. They are briefly described:

➤ **Sāmah:** Mastery over the mind, control over the way of thinking.

➤ **Damah:** Control of external organs like the eyes, the ears, the nose and the like.

➤ **Uparamah:** Observations of one's own duty (*dharma*).

➤ **Titikshā:** Endurance of opposite qualities like cold-heat, pleasure-pain, happiness-sorrow etc.

➤ **Shraddhā:** It is trust in the words of the Vedas (Scriptures) and the teacher.

➤ **Samādhānam:** This denotes having one object (of pursuit) in the mind. It is a distraction-free mind.

The Upanishad is an antidote to narrow outlooks, as it reminds one repeatedly: *"O Immortal One, you do not have this body alone but all the bodies are your body. Leave the idea of the small family, as the whole world is your family. There is none for you to hate as you are in all, and all, including the plants and animal kingdom, exist because of you only."*

Hari Om!

□□□

TOPIC – III
Mundakopanishad

The name *Mundaka* is derived from the ritual known as *sirovrata* – a Vedic vow mentioned in the *Atharva Veda* – in which fire is carried on the head. This indicates renunciation (*sannyāsa*) in which the head is shaved – thus, this Upanishad is also known as *Mundaka* (shaven head).

This ritual has to be performed by those who wish to study the *Atharva Veda* and is a customary ritual for complying with the qualifications required, that is, disciplining of the mind and sense organs.

Mundakopanishad belongs to the fourth Veda (usually designated) and in the last verse it commands that this teaching should not be revealed to those who have not carried out the ritual *sirovrata*. Verses 1.1.6 and 2.3.5 of this Upanishad have been taken for their systematic and logical conclusion in the *Brahma Sutra* – *Samanvaya adhikaranam*.

In this Upanishad, all related issues of Self knowledge have been discussed adequately and clearly and the 'intense desire for liberation (*tivra mumukshatvam*) and speaking of truth' as values have been given predominant importance.

The enquiry of the student has been taken for discussion in a very logical sequence, where the division of knowledge is divided into *parā* and *aparā vidyā*. An elaborate listing of the *aparā vidyā* is brilliantly done, as they should not become a topic of confusion when we move ahead. Similarly, cosmology has also been explained very vividly. The lineage and status description of the teacher and the student is remarkable, where the student is given to visualise his place amongst the luminaries of Vedāntic tradition.

Regarding the text of this Upanishad, each word and sentence is complete in itself though there are two consecutive verses to convey the intent and content. In comparison, the impression cast on the clean slate of the student's mind is very much like that of the *Kathopanishad*. The subject matter of the Upanishad is divided into three chapters and each has two sections. A bird's-eye view of the contents is shown below.

Chapter	Section	Topics
I	1	Glory and overview of teachings to come.
I	2	Material scheme (*aparā vidyā*, the ritual and secular action).
II	1	Brahman as the cause of the Universe – Supreme Knowledge.
II	2	Cause and effect (*Sat* Brahman and the *Chitta Jiva*).
III	1	The preparatory disciplines – emphasis on the value, speaking of truth.
III	2	Discipline and benefit of knowledge of Self (intense desire for liberation highlighted).

TEXT OF THE MUNDAKOPANISHAD
CHAPTER I

Section 1

I.1.1: Brahmā, the creator and protector of this universe, arose as the first among Gods. He expounded the science or knowledge of Brahman (*Brahma vidyā*), the foundation of all knowledge (all sciences) to Atharva, his eldest son.

I.1.2: Tradition of oral communication (teacher and student relationship).

Brahmā (*Creator and protector of the universe*).

↓

Atharva Rishi (*Eldest son of Brahmā. Mānasa putra.*).

↓

Angira Rishi (*An erudite personality and spiritual master*).

↓

Bharadwāja Rishi (*Also known as* satyavāha – *speaker of truth, there is no contradiction between speech, action and thinking*).

↓

Angiras Rishi (*Many mantras are attributed to him* – mantra drashtā. *Teacher in the present context.*).

↓

Shaunaka (*A glorious householder who maintained a great sacrificial hall* – yajna shālā – *and a big kitchen* – pāka shālā).

I.1.3: Shaunaka approached his guru Angiras with humility and some offerings. This conclusively establishes the ancient tradition of transfer of knowledge and a time-tested one, from the teacher to the student through the means of listening. The first teacher of knowledge is the all-powerful, omniscient and omnipotent Lord Himself. (The glory of this knowledge and the teacher is indicated by this narration.) It is of significance to receive Vedic knowledge from the father-cum-teacher. The word *satyavāha* is an indication of the high standard of the student, as adoration to Maharishi Bharadwāja.

In the present context, Shaunaka is the student who had performed several great sacrifices and also fed many people. An approach to the teacher (guru) for *Brahma vidyā* is done with great reverence and humility, as there is no place for ego. The teacher is not approached empty-handed but with some offerings. It is an appropriate convention that when one goes to the temple, to a king or to meet elders, children should carry something to offer. Shaunaka said, *"O master, please teach me about That One, by knowing which everything else stands known."*

I.1.4: The teacher Angiras stated: "Knowledge has two folds and they are known as (1) *Parā Vidyā* – dealing with the higher aspect, the spiritual, and (2) *Aparā Vidyā* – dealing with lower knowledge, matter."

I.1.5: Elaborate details of the lower knowledge or *aparā vidya* are: the first part of the four Vedas itself, namely *Rig, Yajur, Sāma* and

Atharva Vedas along with their six limbs known as *Sikshā* (phonetics), *Kalpa* (codes of rituals), *Vyākarana* (grammar), *Niruktam* (etymology), *Chhandas* (meters), and *Jyothisha* (astrology). The first part of the Vedas is meant to acquire all material gains through rituals. Thus, it shows that all other knowledge of the world comes under *aparā vidyā*. The highest knowledge *parā vidyā* is that knowledge of the Spirit by which the immortal is known.

I.1.6: The very source of all beings, which cannot be seen, known or seized, which has no origin, no properties, which has neither eyes nor ears, neither hands nor feet, which is eternal, diversely manifested, all-pervading, extremely subtle, imperishable and the seers regard It as the source of all beings. In appreciation of the above statement that "It is the source of all beings". In order to show the relationship between the nature of the cause and the nature of the varieties of effects (the products), the Upanishad gives three beautiful analogies.

I.1.7: The **first** analogy is that of the spider and the web it produces. Where and how to make the web and the raw material that goes into making of the web, both have the spider as their cause and in Vedantic terms they are designated as *nimitta* and *upādana kāranam* – intelligent and material cause. So also, the Universe arises from the Immortal without requiring any other cause.

The **second** analogy is that of the earth, which produces innumerable varieties of plants and trees, the one cause that brings out several types of effects.

The **third** example is the human body, which is a living and conscious one producing hair, nails etc that are inert, because of which no pain is experienced when these are cut. This analogy shows the effect of inert things from the cause – Consciousness. These examples speak about the varieties in the effects from the cause. Similarly Brahman, Consciousness, projects the inert Universe. Again, as in the case of the spider, Brahman is both the material and intelligent cause of the Universe.

I.1.8 & 9: Here, how the Universe came into being is described. The relationship between the Universe and Brahman, the cause, is a very important aspect in Upanishadic teachings. It should also be understood that the cause is always present in the effect.

The order of the projection of the Universe is that before manifestation of the Universe, Brahman visualised the need of the Universe and the knowledge about the necessity of enjoyment and sufferings according to the laws of the Cosmos. The 'name' and the form of the Universe already existed but in potential form, just as a seed has all that which goes to form a tree. In the Upanishads, this visualisation by Brahman is said to be the *tapa*, which is the knowledge of what and how to create.

The second stage of the creation is compared to the swelling of the seed. When put under the earth the seed swells before sprouting. It means that the manifestation is about to take place. The third stage is the manifestation of the subtle world, which is compared to the sprout. The next stage is the creation of the visible Universe, which is known as the gross world. It includes the five gross elements known as space, fire, air, water and earth and also the fourteen planets – six above and seven below, including a reference to the one in which beings and plants live.

Section 2

According to the presentation in this Upanishad, this section deals with *aparã vidyã* known as material science – the karma.

Karma has two branches: (a) Karmas in which physical exertion is required and (b) That action which is mind-oriented, also known as meditation – *Upãsanã*.

Again, these actions can be sub-divided into:

➤ All actions performed with a desire to obtain some material gains – known as *kãmya karma*.

➤ Actions performed without any desire or motivation but done to please the Lord only – known as *nishkãma karma*.

I.2.1: In this section dealing with *aparã vidyã* or material science, it is only karmas prescribed in the Vedas along with their limbs (*angas*) that are considered. The common denominator for these two is that one takes the individual more and more into the ephemeral world, whereas the other takes one towards God by ensuring purity of mind.

It should be noted that the same karma performed with two different mental assertions provides entirely two different results or fruits. Each ritual or *upãsanã* blesses the individual

44

with the benefit that accrues thereto. The sacrificial works that the wise found in the mantras of the Vedas are true and were performed with much faith.

I.2.2: In this verse one standard ritual, *agnihotra*, has been taken for discussion, which is very popular and belongs to the part of the daily practice of the three Vedas, namely *Rig, Yajur*, and *Sāma Veda*. The ritual under discussion is a very efficacious time-tested one that is certain to bless a person with results, if performed with faith, following all details and procedures; it is the promise of the Veda.

The description has two-fold information. (1) The actual points where deviations or carelessness are to be guarded against. (2) The intricacies of do's and don'ts are prescribed in such a manner that one should not get over-enthusiastic since this is not the objective of the Vedas.

Next is the location and direction in which the oblations in the *homa kunda* are to be offered – in-between the northern and southern direction, while the doer (the *kartā*) is seated facing the east, after ensuring that the fire has been kindled properly.

I.2.3: Then comes the performance of secondary rituals – on the first moon day (*amāvashyā*), a moon-less night, (*Purnimā*) is full-moon night, the month beginning with *Chaturmasya* rituals etc, as they are part of the main ritual. It is a caution that without these subsidiary rituals the main ritual is not complete, as the desired results are based on meticulous attention to the performance of all these. The Veda also cautions that if it is not performed in proper time, or performed without the rites to Visvadevās, the results will not materialise.

I.2.4-6: The flame in the *homa kunda* has been categorised into seven types of flames, according to the colour and the nature of the flame that emanates at the time of offering oblations and they are given names such as *Kāli* (black one), *Karāli* (terrific one), *Manojavā* (swift as the mind), *Sulohitā* (deep red), *Sudhumra varnā* (smoke-coloured), *Sphulingini* (sparkling) and *Vishvarupi* (having all forms). These flames are considered the tongues of the Fire God (*Agni devatā*), the receiver of the oblations.

Oblations should be offered into properly lit flames and not in their absence. Done according to the injunctions of the Scriptures, the rituals bear two types of results:

(1) When the rituals are performed aiming at fulfilment of a particular desire, the specific desire is fulfilled.

(2) When the ritual is aimed at attaining higher worlds, like *swarga* (heaven), it is attained after death.

The glory of the higher world is described as 'that particular devatā who has been invoked at the time of performing the *agni hotra* ritual and will appear in the form of bright sunrays and guide the soul into *swarga* after death', where a red-carpet welcome is given and praises are offered for the accomplishment. A picturesque account of the royal treatment is given to consider the performance of ritual worthwhile the labour.

I.2.7: Having given the merits of the *Kāmya karma*, the Upanishad now brings out the other side of the coin. The object of praising the performance of rituals is that men will realise the ephemeral nature of worldly and heavenly enjoyments, so as to enable one to choose the courses available. The most important factor one should understand is that all the pleasures attained through rituals are fleeting by nature. The logic advanced is that the means described as the eighteen supporting factors of *agni hotra* in the examples are limited by their very nature and, therefore, the results produced by them are also limited and cannot be infinite. It will be the height of ignorance if one assumes it to be the other way.

I.2.8-10: The Upanishad further cites the folly of the men of rituals who fancy themselves to be wise amongst others and consider themselves torchbearers. Such a person who thinks he has accomplished the goal of life is compared to a blind man leading blind people, as both are groping in the dark with temporary pleasures.

The *agni hotra* ritual is a representative of the rituals and applies to all other Vedic rituals, social services, charity, the building of rest places for pilgrims etc. Criticism is hurled only towards those who perform the rituals with desires and not at those who perform without any worldly desires that will lead oneself to *shukla gati* (the bright path) and attainment of *Brahmaloka*, thereby gain knowledge of the Self and attain liberation. If this option is not exercised, one remains in the ephemeral world.

I.2.11: Having enumerated the unreal, the Upanishad depicts the transition from unreal to real or material knowledge to spiritual knowledge – from *aparā vidyā* to *parā vidyā*. After one has experienced the material world, one understands its drawbacks – that acquiring and preserving is nothing but painful and one should be ready to part with things. The joy is too short and too unreal. Pain is proportionate to the pleasure. Happiness comes in time and also goes away in time. So when one is thoroughly disgusted and disappointed with this nature of happiness, one starts looking for an alternative that is free from all these drawbacks.

I.2.12: Fortunately, one learns there is something that is free from all limitations, known as Brahman. To know the everlasting happiness, revealed only in the Scriptures, and to know and understand its words and sentences, one needs the assistance of a teacher, who can make one understand this unique science. A person wanting to switch over to the science of eternal happiness approaches the preceptor with all humility, according to the prescribed proce-dures and asks to be taught. The preceptor – who is qualified, established in Brahman and has received this knowledge according to the tradition – teaches the disciple whose mind is at rest, with sense organs subdued, and thus is eligible to receive this knowledge.

Thereby, the ideal teacher and the ideal student come together. It is the duty of the teacher to remove all doubts of the student, to teach him the hidden meanings of the

Upanishad and to help him in all possible ways to gain this knowledge.

I.2.13: To that pupil who has approached him respectfully, whose mind is at rest and whose senses are subdued, let the wise teacher truly teach *Brahma vidyā* (science of the Self) through which the true immortal Brahman is known. It is the duty of the teacher to remove all doubts of the disciple, to teach him the hidden meaning of the Vedas and to help him in all possible ways to cross the ocean of ignorance and attain the knowledge of Brahman.

CHAPTER II

Section 1

This section reveals Brahman as the cause of the Universe, so the relation between Brahman and the Universe is the relationship of cause and effect (product). This will be explained with further corollaries.

There are two types of relationship between any cause and effect:

    (a)   The intelligent cause – the maker (*nimitta kāranam*).

    (b)   The material cause (*upādāna kāranam*).

Vedānta recognises Brahman to be both a material and intelligent cause, as was revealed through the example of the spider and the web, but at this point the emphasis is on the material cause. Examples of cause and effect relationship are gold and the ornament, clay and the pot, the ocean and the wave etc.

II.1.1: The Upanishad brings out this relationship with an example of a huge conflagration of fire and the sparks issuing from it. The fire is one and the sparks are many. The characteristics of both heat and light of the fire are also possessed by the sparks, in the same way Brahman is one but the effects are innumerable. The non-essential nature of both the fire and sparks are quite different and not comparable at all and so is the relationship between Brahman, *Jiva* and *Jagat*. The spark goes back into the fire but cannot manifest itself without the presence of the fire.

Now we know that the effect is dependent upon the cause. Again, the cause is in and through the effect, during its creation, existence and its resolution, as the effect goes back into the cause. On the other hand, the cause has independent substance, whereas the effect has no substance at all except the name, form and function, which is not real, being a modification of the cause only, without any reality in itself and is known as *mithyā*. Now the relationship stands as the real *sat* Brahman with that unreal *mithyā jagat* and is the indirect attribute of Brahman.

II.1.2: The next verse is the direct attribute of Brahman, which is a special emphasis to clear the doubt about the cause and effect relationship. Regular examples are that of material to material, whereas Brahman is Consciousness and not inert, as the effect which is unique in Vedānta. Earlier, mention was made of the conscious body which gives room to inert hair and nails. Here, the relation is also from the conscious to the inert.

Under the direct description of Brahman (*swarupa lakshanam*), it is said that the Self-effulgent Brahman is distinctly different from all other things. It is formless, unborn, all-pervading, seated in the city of the body, existing within and without but without mind, *prana* etc, unborn and so undecaying, also immortal and greater than the greatest. Here, the point to ponder is that the name, form and function which are the forms of Brahman and substance-less are actually present in the seed form, just as the lump of clay or gold has all the names and forms but in an unmanifest state. A spherical form is the mixture of all other forms.

II.1.3: The development now is the evolution of the Universe, which we call creation, yet there are no new things – only the projection of the already available one, but in potential form.

The order of evolution or creation of the universe is in four stages: First the five elements (space, air, fire, water and earth) are projected. The second stage is when elementals of these five elements, such as ego and mind consisting of emotion and memory, are brought out. Appearance of the five gross elements by the unification of subtle elements in definite proportion is third in the order. Finally, the gross elements, such as the gross universe, gross body etc, are manifest.

II.1.4: The whole universe is considered to be the body of Brahman in macro vision and compared to the own body at the micro level. Both the universe and our body function as one unit at their level of existence. The *Virat** has come from *Hiranyagarbha** and has features comparable to that of human beings.

For example, the eyes, ears, head, heart, legs at the macro cosmos level. The *Virāt* has three eyes, i.e., sun, moon and fire, to be used in the day or night and when both the sun and moon are not available, fire is to be used. The ten quarters (directions) are the ears, the head is the upper world and the earth is the leg. Consequently, many other things are also born out of *Ishwara* – such as the *jivas*, animals, birds, and other living beings – by different processes of evolution.

II.1.5: Human birth has been explained in *panchāgni vidyā* of the *Chhāndogya Upanishad*, which is described here. The pertinent point in this process is that the forty-first ritual (*antakriyā*) of the one who has led a Vedic life is performed when one leaves the body by offering the gross body to the fire as a final oblation.

Then, in exchange, the Fire God grants another gross body in most subtle form, which undergoes five stages of evolution and the knowledge of these five evolutions is known as *panchāgni vidyā* – knowledge of five fires.

The five stages are:

➤ It goes through heaven, known as *Swargāgni.*

➤ The second stage is through the clouds, known as *parjanya agni.*

---

* See Glossary on pages 117 and 118.

➤ The third stage is through the plant kingdom – *prithvi agni*.

➤ The fourth agni is *reta*, in the form of a seed from the male body – *purusha agni*.

➤ The fifth agni is in the body of a woman that gets transferred from the male body. Thus, the woman brings forth as a baby, with appropriate growth, the full cycle of a human being – *stree agni*.

This is the description of the cycle of birth and death in certain cases. Various rituals and *yajnas* are given to human beings to lead a harmonious existence.

II.1.6: The Veda is the mouthpiece of God and God talks to human beings through this and they alone are given a choice over the types of life to lead, unlike animals that live on instinct and, therefore, do not incur good and bad actions. The three Vedas, *Rig*, *Yajur* and *Sāma*, are meant for the performance of yajnas, pious deeds or sacrificial rituals.

The Upanishad says that the *diksha* (a type of grass called *kusha*) worn by the performer or *kartā* for rituals, his wife, the sacrificial fire, the post to tie the sacrificial animal, sacrificial material used in the *yajna*, the fees (*dakshinā*) given to the priest, the cow given as charity along with the right time and place of performance of the ritual etc have all come from Brahman alone.

Again, the various worlds (*lokas*) which are attained due to the merits of performance, the enjoyment of the benefits that are accrued (heaven and other upper regions) have also come from Brahman alone.

II.1.7: It further continues to give an account of other virtues and various forms of beings that have come from Brahman and have their utility and point of existence in the Cosmic Universe. A few of them are named here. These include heavenly beings, gods of various orders, the injunction for performance, faith in the Scriptures and teachers, grains such as barley and rice used in oblations, the life-force known as *prāna*, cattle, birds, penance and devotion, all the instruments of sacrifices and the code of conduct to be followed.

II.1.8: The Upanishad continues to talk about creation, the effect, which is nothing but an expression of Brahman and the world is only a 'word', a name and form. In this verse there is a description of the items (seven in number), functions and objects and the sensual experiences – two eyes, two ears, two nostrils, a mouth and a tongue.

These have their subtle energy, *indriyas*, the housing known as *Golakam* and the range, *prabhā* and their respective objects of experience. These are compared to a *yajna* – the *golakam* as the *homa kunda*, energy to the flame, and object as the oblation. This *yajna* continues throughout the waking stage only, there is an interval at the time of sleep when these are resolved in the mind.

However, *golakam* is still open but without any transactions – the open counter without an attendant. This makes us understand that we continue to experience Brahman all the time as these are born out of Brahman only and Brahman is expressed through their functions and existence.

II.1.9: Having talked about subjective experiences, the Upanishad further states that from Him proceed the oceans, all the mountains, rivers of every kind and from Him only emanate herbs, juice etc indicating the plant kingdom. The essence, *rasa*, is only responsible to keep the gross and subtle body of the *jivas* together and the *rasa* is only responsible to provide different types of energy required by different functional organs to sustain themselves.

Therefore, the definition of life and death is the association of the subtle and gross body and separation of them respectively.

II.1.10: The verse concludes the topic of creation of the Universe by declaring that Brahman alone is the action of meditation and the result too and those who understand this fact attain liberation. From the essence of all the above descriptions, it is to be concluded and consolidated as the *Sat*, otherwise, 'is'-ness in everything in the world is Brahman and, therefore, Brahman is the only cause of everything to exist thereupon.

Brahman is the one cause and the effects are many. There is no independent existence separate from the effect and so it is *mithyā*. Brahman exists independently and is the substance, and Brahman expresses through the effect, the product, and is present all the time – during origination, existence and destruction. Brahman is the material cause of the world and the world is inert (matter). Brahman is Consciousness and lends its 'is'-ness to all the effects of the world.

There is no world separate from Brahman, as no ornament is separate from gold. The world as we call it is nothing but Brahman. *"Everywhere Brahman alone is"* should be the change in our attitude. *"I am not separate from everything and therefore I am Brahman"*, thus this destroys the knots of ignorance.

Section 2

The previous section enumerated very vividly the material objects that came forth from Brahman-Consciousness with particular reference to the material cause, the *upādāna kāranam* and concluded the identity of Jiva and Brahman as a single entity. In this section, the same idea is further elaborated and, therefore, these verses are known as *mahāvākyam*.

In the first stage, the definition of *Jivatmā* is given. Thereafter, it is described to be one and the same, the *Paramātmā* or Brahman. In the third stage, the glory of this entity, the Ātmā, is revealed with emphasis that one should know that the only knowledge worth knowing, being the real, is this knowledge and all the worlds are, in fact, unreal (*mithyā*).

II.2.1: In the first verse it says that Brahman is bright and near, moving (in the cave of the heart) in the mind, it is great and the supporter of all. All beings that move and breathe are centred in Him. All that is gross (with form) and subtle (formless) is Brahman only. This Brahman is beyond the reach of all the sense organs and that is the *Sat* (existence) and the *Sat* is the *Chitta* (knowledge) and the *Chitta* is the *Sat* – the supporter of all beings. This

Ãtman-Brahman is sought by all beings and the most adorable.

II.2.2: In the second verse, Brahman is said to be the rays of light (awareness), smaller than the smallest and bigger than the biggest; on which all the worlds are founded is this Immortal Brahman. Such are the attributes of Brahman. This very Brahman should be known as the goal of life. The *prāna* (inside) the external speech and mind etc, all are expressions of Brahman only.

II.2.3-4: In the third and fourth verses, the example of an arrow and bow is considered to show the *Jivātmā-Paramātmā* identity. The *Jivātmā* is compared to an arrow, the target being the Brahman. The Shāstra and Veda (OM) are compared to the bow, and the teacher is the unity of the arrow with the bow and the target, which has to be established. The sharpening of the arrow, keeping it straight and pulling back the string to hit the target has been compared to the practice of *sãdhanã.* Keeping the arrow straight on the bow is the development of the personality, known as *arjavam* (consistency between thoughts, speech and action). Pulling back of the string means withdrawing inwardly – that is, no restlessness. Sharpening of the arrow means to keep the intellect sharp through meditation. To keep the attention focused on the target till the arrow is released, to become one with the target and stay put there by getting out of the erroneous notion of separation from Brahman. This fact is to be known by the knowledge imparted through the teachings of the

Upanishads. When the arrow becomes one with the mark, he who aims attains success.

So also, the aspirant who meditates on Brahman attains success or attains the fruit of his meditation. Thus hearing (*sravanam*), reflection (*mananam*) and contemplation (*nididhyāsanam*) have been taught.

II.2.5: The fifth verse talks about the entire eternal creation – that is, the heavens, earth and the intermediary worlds, which are all based upon Brahman only and also the internal worlds, the mind, the *prānas* and the senses. Know Him to be the Self of all and there is no world other than Brahman like there is no ornament other than gold. This has to be grasped. The teacher addresses the disciple: *"This is Self knowledge – the Ātmā and other words are to be discarded in the attempt to attain immortality, to cross the ocean of samsāra."*

II.2.6: The witness principle that is associated with thoughts has been described as the *Ātmā*. The *Ātmā* is one only, though the thoughts are many; deep in an individual or put together, individual thoughts cannot even be counted. The Consciousness that is Awareness handles the thoughts single-handed. It should be clear that thoughts are not Awareness, though it is perceived in the presence of Awareness, which serves as the point of recognisance.

The way it operates is explained, taking the heart as the hub from where all nerves emerge and spread out all over the physical body. The mind rests in the heart and in the mind thoughts arise as well as Awareness, which is witness to the Ātmā. The Ātmā dwells as the silent witness of the three states of Consciousness. The heart is the vital centre where the teacher advises one to meditate upon. Many faculties and attributes are centred in the heart. The student is advised to meditate with the help of *AUM*. In the repetition of AUM there are four stages. *'A'kāra, 'U'kāra, 'M'akāra* and there is a silence before the next repetition and meditating upon the silence is Vedāntic meditation. The teacher emphasises the grasping of that silence, which is Awareness – the Ātmā, the Self. The practice and success in the effort requires the grace of the Lord, guru and shāstra and the teacher grants his blessings to the student for success to cross over from *samsāra* to the shores of Immortal Brahman, which is beyond ignorance.

II.2.7: In the seventh verse, Brahman is defined for the first time, as the *Omniscient Principle* – omniscient from the point of *parā* and *aparā vidyā*. Creation is the glory of Brahman and it is a fact that Brahman alone appears in creation (*vibhuti*). Brahman is discernible more clearly in the temple of the body, that is, in the heart, as Consciousness and enclosed by the mind, known as *daharakasa*, which is pure bliss and immortal. In this way, the immortal Ātmā is seen and worshipped.

II.2.8: The last line of the seventh verse is elaborated upon in the eighth mantra. Here the body is compared to a temple and the heart is the sanctum sanctorum (*garbha griaha*), where Ãtmã or Consciousness resides, which is the *Jivãtmã*. The Ãtmã is described as the leader, which lends its power to the mind and becomes the life of the body and guides the 'vital air' or *prãna* and the body and at the fall of this body enters into another gross body.

The Ãtmã shines in this temple. Though it is all-pervading, it shines forth in the reflecting medium more clearly and powerfully compared to the other medium, where its manifestation is not as intense. Through the eye of knowledge it is recognised as 'witness' – Consciousness – by the competent one, a pure one. The nature of this Self is that it is free from all limitations, and it is eternal. When an aspirant who is free from desires and cravings, has controlled the mind and the senses and is full of discrimination, meditates constantly on Brahman, the knowledge of Self dawns upon him.

The gains from this knowledge are threefold:

➤ Destruction of knots in the heart.

➤ Destruction of doubts about the *Jiva, jagat* and *Ishwara*.

➤ Destruction of karma (*punyam* and *pãpam*) gathered in the past.

The knot is said to be the linking of the Ãtmã with the *anãtmã* and the mistaking of one for the other due to ignorance. Removal of the knots, the ignorance, through the passage of time is impossible and it is attained only by the knowledge of the Self, as described. The experience of the Self, *Ishwara* and the world is quite unbelievable, with reference to the teachings of the Vedãnta.

Vedānta says: "You are Infinite. You are *Ishwara* and the world, which is very evident, is unreal." Doubtless, this understanding is gained. Now the destruction of karma, which is the fruits of actions performed, is explained. There are three types of results gained in any action performed: *prārabdha, sanchita* and *āgāmi*. *Prārabdha* is the name for the effects of one's works, which brought about this birth and have already begun to bear fruit in this life. Accumulated works are known as *sanchita* and current works done in this present life, which will bear fruit in future life, are known as *āgāmi*. On gaining knowledge of the Self, one is insulated from *prārabdha*, *āgāmi* is lost due to loss of ego and *sanchita* gets nullified.

Thus, a *jnāni* with *prārabdha* is known as *jivan mukta* and a *jnāni* without *prārabdha* is known as *videha mukta*, after the fall of the body. These are the benefits of knowledge of the Self – knowledge of Brahman or Ātmā – in the form of cause and effect.

II.2.9: The ensuing verse is also a *mahāvākya*, which reveals the identification of the *Jivātmā* with *Paramātmā* (*samānādhikaranam*). *Paramātmā* is defined as free from any impurities and not subject to impurity at any time. The other definition is that It is without part and division (part and whole philosophy – as applicable to the moon as increase/decrease as 1/15 per day). Therefore, the relationship between the *Jivātmā* and *Paramātmā* cannot be based on the assumption of part and whole, just as with the limbs of the body, as we find our body with so many limbs.

Just as one sees the presence and absence of an object in the constant presence of light, in the same way the sense organs are the light and the light is effective only with the light of the mind. The mind also depends for the light upon another source – 'Awareness'; **Consciousness is the light of all lights that illumines all the other lights.** This light of Consciousness is located in the mind, which is given the title of 'golden case' and sacred 'sanctum sanctorum', where Brahman is present as witness-Consciousness. Whoever thus knows the *Jivātmā* shall know Brahman. Those persons whose minds are impure, whose visions are of an objective nature, cannot realise Brahman.

II.2.10: This verse is an extension of the previous verse, the analysis of light of all lights, presenting different types of illuminators. It says: "The sun does not shine there, neither the moon nor the stars, nor the lightning and much less the fire. When It shines, everything shines after it. By It alone all the lights are illumined."

The essence is that the 'Knower' illuminates all, but none can illumine the Ātmā. The external source of lights, like the sun, the moon and the stars and the internal source of light (illuminator), such as the sense organs, words and the mind cannot illumine the Ātmā, but the Ātmā illumines them all, through the mind and the sense organs. The sense organs illumine external objects from borrowed light – Awareness-Consciousness, which is Ātmā.

'Without the first person, the second and third person cease to exist' is the analogy between the external objects and 'I', the 'Awareness', as without the mind, the sense organs cannot function and without the function of the sense organs, nothing can be perceived. The Ātmā being self-effulgent, it illumines the Self along with the body and this is the cause of mistaking, as we confuse both the Ātmā and *anātmā* and take one for the other.

II.2.11: "I, the Ātmā, am the 'Conscious being' and every other thing is not," is the substance of this verse. The present confusion of seeming duality is removed in the concluding verse, which knocks out the idea and says that Brahman is all-pervading and there is nothing different from Brahman. It says that immortal Brahman is in the front, behind, on the right, on the left, up above and below – all-pervading. Like a dream, everything is itself a dream only, except the waker and so the world is also a dream of the Ātmā only.

CHAPTER III

Section 1

The topics discussed in the third chapter are:

➤ Identity between the *Jivātmā* and *Paramātmā*.

➤ Preparatory disciplines.

➤ The benefits: *Jivan mukti* and *Videha mukti*. The individual is a mixture of two principles.

➤ Consciousness – the Witness.

➤ The *ahamkāra* – the body consciousness.

In fact, Consciousness is neither part/product of the body nor limited by the body; it survives even after the death of the body. Every body consists of the original and reflected consciousness and they are inseparable. The original consciousness is one pervading everything. The reflected consciousness – known as *ahamkāra* or *body consciousness* – is as many as the number of bodies and also subject to modification from body to body and even in the same body.

III.1.1-2: The above is demonstrated by an example in the first verse. On a tree, two birds of the same species are sitting. The bird on the lower branch is eating fruits, some of which are sweet and some bitter, whereas the bird seated on the upper branch keeps watching, doing nothing. The bird on the lower branch is compared to the *body consciousness – Jivātmā* and the one sitting on the upper branch is compared to the *Witness Consciousness* – the *Paramātmā*. The tree is compared to the body-mind complex; fruits are the results of various actions, giving pleasure and pain at variable lengths of time.

The above idea is elaborated in the first two verses indicating that Ātmā is composed of consciousness available in the body as well as Witness Consciousness. When the body consciousness – that is the *Jivātmā* – asserts itself, it is ignorance, depending on external security and enjoying the helplessness, delusion, pain and momentary pleasures.

At some point of time, when the *Jiva* comes across the adorable and noble one, i.e., it wakes up to its higher Self, it is free from the grief of

64

samsãra. The insecurity that gripped one before, no longer exists and it becomes one with the noble, adorable one and free from the fear of mortality. At first, man occupies the place of the bird on the lower branch and later on rises to the higher plane – the witness bird, which is neither a doer nor an enjoyer and also does not have to reap the fruits of actions, as there is no action on its part.

III.1.3: In the next verse also, the *Jiva-Brahman* identity has been talked about. The first line indicates the nature of Brahman and the second line talks about the benefit of this knowledge. The original Consciousness (*Chaitanyam*) and located consciousness are said to be *swarupa lakshanam* and *tatastha lakshanam* – original Consciousness and Witness Consciousness. The distinction is that at the individual level, it is *sãkshi* (witness) and at the world level, it is Brahman, Consciousness being one and the same with two different names. This Consciousness – *Sãkshi* – is the creator, *Hiranyagarbha*, ruler, sustainer and all-pervading and when this Consciousness is owned up (seen as oneself), *Jiva* destroys all merits and demerits and becomes pure from all taints and ignorance.

III.1.4: The succeeding verse also talks about knowledge and its benefits. It says that the wise know that *prãna* is the Lord appearing in all living beings. Here *prãna* indicates Brahman. Ãtmã blesses the *prãna* that is lent to the body. The realised one sees Brahman everywhere and in everyone since he himself is so complete and content and maintains silence. He is absorbed in Brahman and always engaged in the service of society. His very presence in society is the source of inspiration and he is the greatest among persons.

III.1.5-6: In the two ensuing verses, the required disciplines are talked about for knowledge of the Self. The disciplines are truthfulness (avoidance of speaking untruth), penance (*tapas*), application of senses and mind, sexual chastity (*brahmacharya*), proper enquiry through shāstra and guru (*samyak jnānam*) etc. This enquiry will be fruitful only when impurities of the mind become weak and the only goal in life becomes liberation from the ocean of *samsāra*, with no other pursuit. Then the discovery is the *Self-effulgent Ātmā* – Pure Consciousness within the body and mind. The highlight in these verses is the virtue of speaking the truth, amongst other virtues.

The popular phrase *satyameva jayate* is from this verse itself. This verse emphasises that speaking the truth is absolutely necessary for liberation and this virtue alone may have an edge over other virtues to attain *Brahmaloka* through the bright path (*shukla gati*) after death. It says – *Satyameva jayate* (Truth alone triumphs).

Speaking the truth is the basic tenet even for meditation. Truth must be understood as not speaking lies. It adds that those with a burning desire for liberation who cannot get an opportunity for the proper means to attain it may also go to *Brahmaloka*, if associated with speaking the truth. One who rigorously follows the virtue of speaking the truth shall attain liberation in stages (*karma mukti*). The essence of this portion is that without relative truth, the Absolute Truth (Brahman) cannot be realised.

III.1.7: Sharp intellect is an aid to cognise subtle elements. Therefore, the *sādhaka* must be equipped with this accessory to know the subtle Ātmā. It emphasises that one requires subtle and sharp intellect to know the Ātmā. The equipment may be seen here as the fourfold qualifications (sense and mind purity).

Here the nature of Ātmā is explained:

➤ **Infinite (limitless):** In fact, the property of subtlety is proportionate to the vastness. For example, among the five gross elements, space (*ākāsha*) is subtler than either water or earth and among the five it is the most subtle. In this case, space is in Brahman and, therefore, it is much more subtle than any other element.

➤ **Self-evident (*divyam*):** Ever the subject and never an object, self-luminous.

➤ **Inconceivable (*achintya*):** Beyond imagination, cannot be objectified, unthinkable.

➤ **Most subtle (*sukshmati sukshmatram*):** Subtler than the most subtle, appears as everything.

➤ **Farther (*durāt–sudoora*):** It is farther than the farthest because it is Infinite, it cannot be understood by the ignorant.

➤ **Nearer (*antika*):** Brahman is shown as 'nearer than the nearest' – present in one's own mind and pervading everything. He dwells in the heart. It indicates that it is very near to those who have realised Brahman.

➤ **Sat and chit:** The very witness of every thought and also in the absence of thoughts.

The very intent of the sharpness of mind means dropping the idea of expectations to experience Brahman. Brahman is not a particular experience but through and through every experience.

III.1.8: In the previous verse, the subtlety of Brahman was narrated. In this verse, the Upanishad asserts that subtle intellect is required to realise the Brahman. The topic is designed in two folds.

➤ What cannot reveal Brahman.

➤ What can reveal Brahman.

It says the eyes cannot reveal Brahman and, in the same way, words too cannot describe It, as the Ātmā is subtle, formless and beyond any description. In *Kenopanishad*, the teacher asserts that whatever you see or hear is not Brahman but something else. The same idea is applied here too. Only two sense organs have been talked about but it is applicable to all the sense organs.

It further says that austerity (*tapas*) cannot reveal Brahman, as also rituals and other actions. *Sādhanas* like austerity and rituals are not useful in revealing Brahman. At the same time, these are very useful in preparing the mind and sense organs towards purity and subtlety.

Ātmā/Brahman can be revealed by the Scriptures (*shāstra*) alone, for which the mind must be made suitable to assimilate. What is the mind that can reveal? It is that mind which has been purified by cleansing it of desires and aversion. The mind that is refined and tuned to subtlety alone can have blessings for knowledge, which is listening, thinking and contemplation. The sense/mind that has been blessed with fourfold qualifications (*sādhana chatushthaya sampati*) alone can know the indivisible, pure and subtle Brahman.

III.1.9: The ninth verse again consolidates the idea of the subtle mind and subtle Brahman. The mind which is available in the body is sentient because there are five *prānas* (*prāna*, *apāna*, *udāna*, *vyāna* and *samāna*), the physiological energy that keeps the body alive. The body is alive because of *prāna* and *prāna* is available because of *Chaitanyam* that pervades the mind along with thoughts and this *Chaitanyam* (Consciousness) is self-evident. In the mind that is relatively less crowded with thoughts, Consciousness is more evident.

III.1.10: In the last verse of this section, a *jnāni* (man with knowledge of the Self) is glorified. The knower, who has recognised the Infinite Brahman, the substratum of the entire creation, pure and luminous, knows that *"I am that Infinite Brahman".*

The glorification is done in two ways:

➤ Glorification of Ãtmā (*Ishwara–jnāni* identity).

➤ Glorification of *anātmā* (introducing the guru and the student, which is in the relative plane.)

The question is – can the *jñāni* and *Ishwara* be identical from the plane of *anātmā*? Literally, it is not possible, but the Scripture rather affirms that due to extraordinary purity in the person with knowledge of the Self, and in the absence of ego, the manifestation of *Ishwara* is more and capable of fulfilling prayers for material and spiritual desire.

The *jñāni* is compared to a temple where the manifestation of the Lord is more compared to other places. The Lord blesses the individual through the *jñāni*, as the prayer goes to the Lord only, as a *jñāni* is without any ego – *ahamkāra* – and so he becomes a channel to the Lord in the form of the guru tradition and the Lord Himself is the first guru.

In this verse, though fulfilment of material desires is mentioned, the next section talks about the spiritual gain that is bestowed upon the individual through the *jñāni*.

Section II

III.2.1: This section also continues with the glory of the knowledge of the Self. Wise men who understand the *jñāni* as the supreme Brahman, supporter of the universe and worship Him without any desire for materialistic pleasures, attain immortality. One should not mistake this fulfilment through touchstone from the *jñāni*, but the *jñāni* imparts spiritual knowledge to the desirous systematically, which alone leads to liberation.

III.2.2: The second verse indicates that this knowledge can destroy rebirth and lead to liberation and the mechanism is explained. It is accepted that desire leads to action, which leads to result, result goes to character and character makes one concentrate with a singular thought at the time of death and that obsession alone decides the next birth to fulfil the agenda of the previous birth. A *jñāni* has no desire to be fulfilled and the desirelessness leads to liberation from rebirth. Those who are left with any particular desire are born again to fulfil that desire, which are of various types, and so there are various *lokas* (worlds) and wombs to get a suitable body.

III.2.3: This verse explains the requirements to know and realise the Ātmā. The Upanishad says there should be intense desire and not merely the study of Scriptures, intelligence and retention power. One must have the thirst for final emancipation; the intense yearning and a burning desire for the objective and be prepared for any sacrifice, since *Paramātmā* reveals the knowledge only to the sincere seeker. In fact, liberation is not a thing to be achieved or produced. It is already there, but only the ignorance has to be dispelled to own up the true Self and realise the very nature that is Ātmā.

III.2.4: The next verse compliments the previous one, emphasising in double negative the qualifications and preparative means required to realise Brahman.

It highlights four qualifications:

➤ Will power – indicating intellectual strength.

➤ Alertness – not losing sight of the goal.

➤ Austerity and knowledge – indicating enquiry into the Scriptures under a teacher.

➤ Determination and detachment – growing out.

The Ãtmā cannot be realised by one who is destitute of strength or without earnestness and penance. The point is that all these should be in full measure for knowledge of the Self.

III.2.5: In the fifth verse, the benefit of knowledge of the Self is given in two stages: *Jivan mukti* – inner freedom while living, and *Videha mukti* – freedom attained after death. The process is not a sudden consequence but takes time, that too in stages, from gross level to subtle level.

The seeker goes through various stages and refinement takes place gradually as under:

➤ Recognition of the fact that the spiritual goal is the ultimate.

➤ Getting detached – except liberation all other things are secondary in life.

➤ Tranquillity – no more restlessness of the mind. Becoming an introvert.

➤ Acquiring knowledge through systematic and consistent study under a competent teacher.

➤ Understanding that *Jivātmā* is none other than the *Paramātmā*. Changing the misconception.

➤ Having recognised the nature of the Self, becoming ever satisfied, despite surroundings, due to the change in vision – *Jivan mukti*.

➤ Continuing in the knowledge, without slipping down, constantly dwelling on Brahman.

➤ At the time of leaving the body, the seeker merges into the all-pervading Brahman totally – *Videha mukti* pervades the whole creation – identity with Brahman.

It is similar to educational qualifications. One does not become a graduate overnight. The stages of attainment in the pursuit of a religious life-style are also similar. One becomes a *dhira* (an accomplished soul), a man of knowledge of the Self and gets devoid of attachment. Passion drops down and one begins discarding petty things and resorts to *Jnãna Yoga* – realisation of the Supreme Self.

The essential nature of a *Jivan mukta* is mentioned as one who is:

➤ *Jnãna triptah* – satisfied with the knowledge.

➤ *Kriyãtmanah* – who has realised the Atma.

➤ *Vitarãgah* – devoid of attachment.

➤ *Sarvaga* – all-pervading.

➤ *Dhira* – the wise.

III.2.6: The sixth verse presents some more stages a seeker will go through in becoming a *jnãni*. He has a pure mind in which only legitimate likes and dislikes reside. He has balance of mind and such a person becomes a committed pursuer of knowledge. His primary duty in life is only to gain the ultimate knowledge. Such a person becomes wise – knowing clearly the teachings of the Upanishad.

As a result of this knowledge, he attains identity with Brahman and wakes up to his immortal nature. He is like the 'pot space' while living and merges with Brahman, just as 'pot space' becomes one with the *ākāsha* when it breaks. He attains a final death, as there is no more rebirth for him.

III.2.7: Merger of the individual soul into the total is explained in the seventh verse. The microcosm of body of the *jnani* is compared to fifteen parts of the moon, so also the macrocosm. At the end of the *prarabdha*, the parts of the *jnani* merge into the total. These include the causal and the subtle body – the energy into the total (*adhishtana devata*) and so all become one, losing the separate identity. All three types of karmas – *sanchita, agami* and *prarabdha* – are not retained but merge into *Ishwara* – the total, including the 'I' notion, which is in the waking stage alone. This happens only in the case of a *jnani*.

III.2.8: The above concept is beautifully explained in the eighth verse with the example of rivers merging into the ocean. The different names, forms and sizes that the rivers have are lost totally and become one when they join the ocean and remain there as water, the essential substance, which is one and the same in both. The original source of the river is the ocean only, but is mistaken as the mountains, these being the immediate cause.

Similarly, the Jiva is not anything different except the name and form with its essential nature of Consciousness, which is the Ātmã,

74

the substance of all sentient and insentient things. Name and form is lost but the substance is not lost.

III.2.9: In this verse too, the topic of *jivan mukti* and *videha mukti* is continued. The knowledge of the Self has been glorified as the "knower of Brahman becomes Brahman". This concept creates doubt that the 'knower of one thing becomes that' and is a serious problem when applied to other objects of the relative world. The idea is that there is no question of 'becoming', as 'it' is already there – only the wall of ignorance stands, which separates the two, otherwise it has two names only.

Logic holds that a finite thing cannot become infinite. At best it can be another finite only but not infinite. This is possible only under one condition. *"I am already Brahman but ignorant about it."* So the very knowledge makes one free from *samsāra*, one who is beyond good and bad. The whole Vedānta is one of knowing and owning up.

The Upanishad says that for such a person the knots of the heart are broken. The knots of the heart imply ignorance that binds one to the cycle of birth and death. Such a person faces no obstacles in his march towards the goal. It is further glorified that not only does he become a *jnāni*, he also converts others into *jnānis* and no members of his family, if he is a householder, or no disciple, in the case of a *gurukula*, remains ignorant any more. At the end of *prārabdha* he gets *videha mukti*.

75

III.2.10-11: The last two verses of the Upanishad talk about appropriate fitness to receive knowledge of the Self from the teacher. For any seed to sprout and become a tree, a proper fertile ground is necessary. Whatever the quality of the seed, it will not germinate to make good the shortcomings of the soil.

In this case, the mind of the student must be pure, the intellect should be sharp, and the senses should be under restraint, besides having dispassion and discrimination, the fourfold qualities known as *sādhanā chatushtaya sampati*. To obtain the necessary qualifications, *karma yoga* and *upāsanā* have been prescribed.

This Upanishad belongs to *Atharva Veda* and it quotes a mantra from the *Rig Veda*. It says the student must study the Scriptures regularly and practise the prescribed disciplines for spiritual growth – the *Pancha yajna* (*karma yoga*). He must also show commitment to the pursuit of Brahman and practise certain special rituals prescribed for students to study the *Atharva Veda* – namely *Ekādashi vratam*, have faith in the efficacy of the rituals and practise another ritual known as *Shirovratam*. The Upanishad says that this teaching should be given only to students with a purified mind. It emphasises that before taking up *nirguna Brahma sādhanā*, one must have had the *saguna Brahma upāsanā* – the rituals of *karma kānda*.

The Upanishad concludes that this teaching was given thousands of years ago by the teacher Angiras to Maharishi Shaunaka. Though a very ancient teaching, it is valid even today. It will be beneficial only when these disciplines are followed. At the end there is *guru paramparā*, where the student prostrates twice, first to show gratitude and devotion towards the guru and the second time, the repetition marks the conclusion of the teachings of the Upanishads.

Hari Om!

❑❑❑

TOPIC – IV
Principal Upanishads

The following nine Upanishads, along with
Mundakopanishad discussed earlier, contain
almost all the topics of the 108 Upanishads.
Vyāsāchārya's Brahma-Sutras find relevance
from these Sutras and Shri Shañkarāchārya has
taken verses for his commentary on Brahma-
Sutra as *Shruti-Pramānam*.

Ishāvāsya Upanishad:

This Upanishad belongs to the Shukla Yajur
Veda, like Brihadāranyaka Upanishad. This is
Mantropanishad, whereas Brihādaranyaka
Upanishad is a commentary on Ishāvāsya. Since
this Upanishad is in the mantra part of this Veda,
ritualists claim it to be part of the *Karma*, rituals
and sacrifices, whereas these are negated by the
Vedāntins. To establish that it has no relation
with *Karma,* as it is established that there is no
linga or *Shruti-Pramānam* to that effect. There
is a big argument for and against this proposition.

This Upanishad teaches to renounce name, fame
and form to enjoy the Bliss, *Brahmānanda*. Do
the actions without a selfish aim, so that it does
not bind one. Brahman is one that is motionless,

near, and far off, not tainted by the attributes, immanent and transcendental and dwells in all the hearts. All these descriptions above are of *Jivātmā*, which is nothing but Paramātma, it proves that this Upanishad is Vedānta oriented. But ritualists say that all these are flowery words, only glorifications, merely to please the *kartā*, the doer, but it is not true. The Vedāntic essence is that the God is in-dweller in everything. Shri Shankarāchārya brings out that the Isāvāsya mantras do not prove the descriptions of the Ātma as the doer or experiencer and of not even the beneficiary of any actions; thus this cannot be a part of *Karma-Kānda*. Thus it is concluded that it cannot be assigned to the rituals but to *Jnāna-Kānda*, that deals with the statement of facts- the means for knowledge, that knowledge which is liberation-*moksha*.

Kenopanishad:

Ken Upanishad is a smaller one, containing four chapters only, which is in prose form. This is Brāhmanopanishad. Here the first word is *'Kena'* and so the Upanishad is called 'Kenopanisd'. The meaning of the word *'kena'* is 'by whom'. Shānti-pātha' of this Upanishad is that of the respective Veda, which is Sāma-Veda and is chanted in the beginning by both the teacher and the student together, to ward off the obstacles arising out of self, surrounding and divine dispensation (supernatural forces). There must be a teacher and a disciple as there are questions to seek clarifications. The student has the knowledge that the body is matter (inert). Second point is that even the subtle body including mind is made up of matter only and the student has observed that the body mind-complex behaves like sentient one. The question is that the insentient body-mind – complex becomes sentient for which there must be some cause to activate them, so the invisible principle is named as Deva. The teacher answers to this question that this principle is Ātmā.

First two parts deal with the nature of Brahman as the Brahman is the 'eye of eye, ear of ear and mind of mind'. Eye, ear and mind cannot comprehend by themselves, but for the presence of Ātmā – the Brahman. Again Brahman is not an object but always the subject.

The third part is presented in the form of a dialogue between the *Devas* and *Yaksha*, to remove the pride of the *Devas*, who took the credit to themselves for winning over the *asuras*. It is a prelude to bring the teacher and the taught together. Umādevi appears as the teacher and Indra as the student as the *deva* too had to be taught the *'Brahma-vidyā'*.

The fourth part is about the meditation on the Brahman and the benefits of such meditation. When actions are done without expectations of results, lead to purification of the mind but it cannot lead to liberation. Brahman is birth less as well as free from of modifications and is beyond time, space and qualities.

Kathopanishad:

This is one of the most beautiful and popular Upanishad. Some understand this as 'Kata' for 'Katha', which is derived from the recension of

Krishna Yajurveda - Taittiriya Brāhmana. The sublime doctrine of the Vedānta, presented in this Upanishad is very attractive and appealing. This has won the appreciation of many inquirers, including French and German scholars. It is one of the best books on Vedānta philosophy and poetry of ancient Hinduism. Swami Vivekananda often used to quote from this Upanishad. No other Upanishad has so much of thought elevation, depth of expression, and beauty of imaginations that this Upanishad possesses.

One such expression, to quote is the comparison of the body with chariot, in which the soul is the Lord of the chariot, intellect is the charioteer, mind is the rein, the five sense organs are compared to the horses, and the road is the sense objects. This Upanishad has the answers to the profound questions of mystery:

➤ What is left after death?

➤ What is beyond merits and demerits?

It forms the central theme of this Upanishad.

Prashnopanishad:

Prashna Upanishad belongs to Atharva Veda and the other two Upanishads belonging to this Veda are Mundaka and Māndukyopanishad. Prashnopanishad belongs to the Brāhmana portion of the Veda, whereas Mundaka is of the *mantra bhāga*. Thus Prashnopanishad is the commentary on Mundakopanishad, as the scriptural tradition is. *Karma, upāsanā* as well as *Parā-vidyā* have been dealt with, in this Upanishad, which had been hinted in Mundaka. The first chapter deals with the two paths [*gati*], which have been mentioned in Mundaka as *Krishna gati and Shukla gati*.

The second and third chapters expand the talks on *upāsanā, Prāna upāsanā* and *aparā-vidayā*. The fourth chapter deals with *Parā-vidyā* through *Sushupti*. Fifth chapter explains *'Omkāra'* *upāsanā* through meditation on individual letters as well as one word. As an answer to the sixth question, *Parā-vidyā* is discussed through the sixteen *kalās*. The *kalās* are *prāna,* faith, *ākāsha,* air, fire, water, earth, senses, mind and food, from food strength, penance, *mantras, karma,* world and the words, and names. These *kalās* are super-imposed, to be eliminated through *'neti, neti'*.

This Upanishad is named as Prashnopanishad as each topic is dealt through questions by six students and the answers to these are given by Pippalāda, the great sage.

Māndukyopanishad:

Māndukya Upanishad is the smallest among the ten Upanishads. This Upanishad too belongs to Atharva Veda. The name has been derived from the name of the sage Manduka, who was supposed to be always happy. This Upanishad has twelve verses only. In Muktikopanishad, which is in dialogue form between Shri Rāma and Hanumānji, says that study of Māndukya Upanishad, comprehensively is sufficient to lead one to liberation. If one is not able to understand, then one has to study either ten or thirty two or one hundred and eight Upanishads. The great sage Gaudapāda has written commentary on this

Upanishad. He gives him a place in the *guru-paramparā*, beginning from Shri Nārāyana. The *paramparā* up to Shuka is mythological *paramparā* and they were *grihasthas,* after him it is history only. Gaudapāda was a sanyāsin, who was the *parama-guru* of Shri Shankarāchārya. He is supposed to have lived in Gauda desha, which might have been in Bengal. Adding the word 'pāda' with the name indicates reverence.

The commentary written by Gaudapāda is called *'kārikā',* which is in verse form and it has 227 verses and each verse is called a *kārikā.* The Upanishad and *kārikā* are to be studied together, which was initiated by Srî Shañkarāchārya. These 227 verses have been divided into four *prakaranas* [chapters] namely *'āgama, vāitasya, advaita and alāta-shānti.*

The *Shānti-pātha* is the same as the *Shānti-pātha* of Upanishads of Atharva Veda. In the prayer, the student asks for allotted life and then for health along with proper functioning of sense organs and also to see and think only auspicious things.

The first chapter is devoted to Upanishad, which is in prose form. First mantra is devoted to enquiry on 'Omkāra, to bring out the ultimate Truth, whereas the second mantra deals with enquiry on Ātmā. Mantras 3 to 7, are elaboration of the second mantra. The sacred syllable 'Om' is glorified as the entire creation, so by studying 'Om', one is studying the whole world, including all the past, present and the future creations and also anything which is beyond time. Consciousness [Brahman] is beyond time.

Aitereyopanishad:

Aitereya Upanishad is also one among the ten Upanishads, which have been commented by Shri Shankarāchārya and this is the only Upanishad, belonging to Rig Veda, among the ten. This is to show that all the four Vedas uniformly propound Vedānta – "*Brahma satyam – jagan mithyā*". Mantras from all the ten Upanishads have been taken in Brahma-sutra for analysis of the six topics of enquiry, namely '*Jiva, jagat, Ishvara*, bondage, liberation and means of liberation. Kaushitaki Upanishad too belongs to Rig Veda and though no commentary of Shri Shankarāchārya is available on it but he has quoted from it.

This Upanishad is in the *āranyaka* of the Veda, the end portion. It has its importance to represent the '*mahā-vākya*' – '*Prajnānam Brahma*'. This Upanishad is attributed to sage Mahidāsa Aitereya. The story goes that he was the son of Itarā, which means the other wife. Another meaning is low caste woman, as he had Mahidāsa along with his name. His mother prayed to goddess Earth and so he was placed in a celestial seat and was imparted this Upanishadic wisdom. The teaching is as sublime as in other Upanishads.

This Upanisad has three chapters, the first chapter has three sections, second has one and the third has one. In the first chapter the non-dual Brahman is revealed through Cosmology [*adhyāropa – apavāda*]. In the second chapter we get the various stages of *Jiva* – right from *garbhā-vāsa* – from the womb. While teaching the second chapter, it is mentioned that 'pregnant women should withdraw', which indicates that ladies were also studying *Brahma-vidyā*. Third chapter is the essence of *'mahā-vākya'* : identity with the Brahman. This Upanishad has its own *shāntipātha* to ward off the three types of obstacles.

Taittiriya Upanishad:

This Upanishad belongs to Krishna Yajur Veda and included in *'Āranyaka'* portion. The legend goes to describe that Yājnavalkya was the disciple of sage Vaisampāyana. At one time Yājnavalkya misbehaved with one of his colleagues that displeased his mentor and he asked him to vomit out what he had learned from him, since the teachings have not blessed him. Yājñavalkya was an obedient student, who vomited all that he learnt along with the food he had eaten. Thus the others got an opportunity to assimilate the knowledge easily without putting effort for it. They took the form of the bird named *'Tittar'* and picked up the vomit to gain the knowledge. This is only a symbolic expression, as he might have been asked to teach his co-students, he being a bright student himself. Thus this knowledge is put in 'Taittiriya Shākhā', wherein there is Taittiriya Brāhmana, Āranyaka and Taittiriya Upanishad, just as Kātha-Shākhā has Kathopanishad.

Taittiriya Upanishad has three chapters, known as *'valli'* [creeper]. First chapter has the name *'Sikshāvalli'* as the chapter starts with the word *'Sikshā'*. The second chapter is known as *'Brahma Valli'* or *'Brahmānanda-valli'* as the the chapter starts with the word 'Brahma', whereas the third chapter starts with the word 'Bhrigu' and is called

'*Bhrigu-valli*'. First chapter deals with *Upāsanās* and it is '*sādhanā-pradhāna*' and the second and third chapters teach '*Brahma-vidyā*'.

In the first chapter the students are leaving for home, after the completion of '*Guru-kula-vāsa*'. The teacher advises the students to keep the fire of values burning in their day-to-day life, like speaking truth and following righteousness etc.

Revelation of Brahman through the analysis of the five sheaths-*annamaya, prānamaya, manomaya, vijnānamaya* and *ānandamaya koshas* is the second chapter. An important note is the chanting method of Taittiriya which is still preserved and also for Brihadāranyaka and Ishāvāsya, but rarely used.

Chhāndogya Upanishad

Chhāndogya means the singer of Veda, or the person belonging to Sāma-Veda. Sāma means '*samatvam*' or 'harmony'. This Upanishad has eight chapters, and each chapter has been divided into sections called '*Khanda*'. First five chapters deal with *upāsanās* only and also the seventh chapter. The sixth chapter is known as '*sat-vidya*' where the *mahā-vākya* '*tattvamasi*' occurs and also this chapter is taken as a model for determining the central theme of the scriptures as given by the *mimāmsā shāstra. Udgita* is the mountain peak of Sāma-Veda.

The student in his prayer seeks fitness of body and mind complex, faith and the four fold qualifications for the study of *Vedānta*. First mantra is the introduction for enquiry into 'AUM', which is the *upāsanā* for achieving quietitude of mind and sharpening the intellect – mental exercise – a symbol used for meditation. Here the sāma-Veda is taken as a symbol for the very reason that the student would have been constantly studying the Sāma-Veda mantra. *Udgita* is the particular *upāsanā* of Sama-Veda / Chhāndogya.

Highlights of the Upanishad : 'AUM' is everything. *Prāna* as *devatā* in *udgita upāsanā*, earth is the Veda and Veda is seen on the body. Imaginary contest for supremacy between sense organs, Ushasti – the *Siddha upāsakā* of Sāma-Veda, another *sādhaka* by the name *Bakā*, who has been instructed by a sage for creating food through Sāma mantra *upāsanā* are some of the legends. *Prāna* is the oldest and best among the senses at macro as well as micro level. There are many legends to teach *upāsanā* and the later part is *Brahma-vidyā*. Chhāndogya Upanishad is very important for the study of Brahma-sutra as Chhāndogya mantra is quoted for almost all the sutras as *shruti-pramānam*.

Brihadāranyaka Upanishad:

This Upanishad belongs to Shukla Yajur-Veda, Kanva-Shākhā. The other Shākhā is Madhyāndina Shākhā. This Upanishad is available in both the Shākhās with slight difference in the text. The contents have been divided into three divisions, each one is known by the name *khanda*. The first *khanda* is known as *Madhu Khanda*, the second division is called *Muni* or *Yājnavalkya khanda* and the third one is called *Khila khanda*. *Madhu khanda* has *upadesha* as primary aim [teaching of Brahman].

In this, Brahman is revealed as the substratum of interdependence, which is discussed by the special word 'madhu'. The second *Khanda* is devoted to Yājnavalkya and is for *mananam*. Throughout this *khanda*, Yājnavalkya is the teacher with different disciples. Most of the Shukla Yajur-Veda is known to be belonging to Yājnavalkya. He is known by another name 'Vājasaneyi', because his teacher happens to be Surya-devatā and Surya-devatā is called 'Vājasaneya', and Shukla Yajur-Veda is also known as 'Vājasaneya samhitā'.

The third division *Khila khanda* contains varieties of *upāsanās* and *karmas*. The meaning of 'khila' is compilation. It is a mixture of several topics and not systematically organized. Each khanda is divided into two chapters, thus six chapters in all, and each chapter has several sections, known as Brāhmana.

The meaning of the word 'Brihad', is big and this Upanishad is relatively big both in content and quality. Both Brihadāranyaka and Chhāndogya have almost same number of pages, but Brihadāranyaka has more contents. Chhāndogya has more number of *upāsanās*, whereas Brihadāranyaka deals with Vedānta in full. It is called 'āranyaka' because its target is on those, who opt for 'vānaprastha', the third stage of life. The substance of *upāsanā* and *Vedānta* prepares one for the last of the *āshrama-dharama*, the *sanyāsa*. *Sanyāsis*, learning from *sanyāsi*, a matured person is *āranyaka*. Upanishad is the remover of pain and grants fulfillment. The *Bhāsyam* written by Shri Shankarāchārya on this Upanishad is the greatest in volume and substance. Sureshāchārya, his disciple has written commentary *Bhāsyam* on this, which is known as 'Vārtikā'. It is bigger, having about 12,000 verses. A number of books have been written by many āchāryas on the text of Brihadāranyaka.

'*Sambandham Bhāsyam*' is the introductory work on this Upanishad by Shankarāchārya, which is the relationship between *karma* and *jnāna*. Some topics, we find, are repeated, For example, teachings of Yājnavalkya to Maitreyi appear both in *Madhu* and *Muni khanda*. This Upanishad is of great value to sanyāsis.

Highlights : One may meditate upon the horse, to be offered in ashvamedha yajna, by thinking that it is Prajāpati, the Lord of beings. This *upāsanā,* which can be practiced even by those, who are not competent to perform *ashvamedha* sacrifice and that grants the same benefits as the very sacrifice itself.

Hari Om!

◻◻◻

TOPIC – V

Important Verses

Some of the most popular verses of the Upanishad are given in this chapter, which should be committed to memory as they represent the concept of Upanishadic teachings and are effective in inspiring us in our daily life. The idea of some of the verses is repeated in the other Upanishads also, which underlines their importance. They have also been the source for the *Shrimad Bhagavad Gitā*, especially many verses from the *Kathopanishad*, which have been incorporated into the *Bhagavad Gitā*.

The Upanishads from the four Vedas uniformly teach *Brahma vidyā* and there is no contradiction in their theme and the essence.

शौनको ह वै महाशालोऽङ्गिरसं विधिवदुपसन्नः पप्रच्छ ।
कस्मिन्नु भगवो विज्ञाते सर्वमिदं विज्ञातं भवतीति । ।3 । ।

Shaunaka, the great teacher, approached Angiras in the manner laid down by the Scriptures and questioned: "What is that, O Bhagavan, which being known, all this becomes known?"

–Mundaka 1-1-3

"That teaching by which what is never heard becomes heard, what is never thought of becomes thought of, what is never known becomes known? Sir, what is that teaching?"

–**Chhandogya Upanishad 6-1-3**

The disciple asks: "Who impels the mind to alight on its objects? At whose command does prāna proceed to function? At whose command do men utter speech? What intelligence directs the eyes and the ears towards their respective object?"

–**Kenopanishad 1-1**

यत्तददेश्यमग्राह्यमगोत्रमवर्णमचक्षुः श्रोत्रं तदपाणिपादम् ।
नित्यं विभुं सर्वगतं सुसूक्ष्मं तदव्ययं यद्भूतयोनिं परिपश्यन्ति धीराः । ।6 । ।

That which cannot be seen or seized, which has no origin, which has no properties, which has neither eyes nor ears, which has neither hands nor feet, which is eternal, diversely manifested, all-pervading, extremely subtle and imperishable, the wise regard as the source of all beings (Bhutas or all creations).

–**Mundaka 1-1-6**

The Self cannot be reached by speech, by mind, or by the eyes. How can it be realised otherwise, other than from those who say, "He is."

–**Kathopanishad 2-6-11**

His form is not to be seen. No one beholds Him with eye. By controlling the mind, by the intellect and by incessant meditation He is revealed. Those who know this Brahman become immortal.

–**Kathopanishad 2-6-9**

I know this ancient one who is free from decrepitude, who is the Self of all, and who is omnipresent by virtue of pervasiveness; regarding whom the deliberators on Brahman speak of birthlessness, and whom they speak of as eternal.

–Shvetāsvatara Upanishad 3-21

यथोर्णनाभिः सृजते गृह्गते च यथा पृथिव्यामोषधयः सम्भवन्ति ।
यथा सतः पुरुषात्केशलोमानि तथाक्षरात्सम्भवतीह विश्वम् ।।7।।

As the spider sends forth and draws in its web, as herbs grow from the earth, as hair grows from the living man, so this universe proceeds from the Immortal Brahman.

–Mundaka 1-1-7

As the spider weaves out the web and again withdraws it, so the Jiva comes out to and goes back again to the wakeful and dreaming states respectively.

–Brahmopanishad

परीक्ष्य लोकान् कर्मचितान् ब्राह्मणो निर्वेदमायान्नस्त्यकृतः कृतेन ।
तद्विज्ञानार्थं स गुरुमेवाभिगच्छेत् समित्पाणिः श्रोत्रियं ब्रह्मनिष्ठम् ।।22।।

Let an aspirant after he has examined the world gained by karma, acquire freedom from all desires, reflecting that nothing that is eternal can be gained by karma. Let him, in order to obtain the knowledge of the eternal, take sacrificial fuel (samid) in his hands and approach that preceptor alone who is versed in the Vedas and established in Brahman.

–Mundaka 1-2-12

The good and the pleasant take hold of man; the wise man examines and distinguishes them. The wise man prefers the good (shreya), but the ignorant man chooses the pleasant (preyas) *for the sake of the body.*

–Kathopanishad 1-2-2

Nachiketā said: "These things last till tomorrow (ephemeral) O Death; they wear out the vigour of all the senses. Even the longest life is verily short. Keep thou thy chariots, the dance and music."

–Kathopanishad 1-1-25

The ignorant run after external objects of desire and fall into the snares of widespread death; but wise men, knowing the nature of immortality, do not covet the fleeting (unstable) thing here.

–Kathopanishad 2-4-2

Seek the enlightenment by prostrating, by questions and by service; the wise, the seers in the Truth will instruct you into the knowledge.

–Bhagavad Gitā 4-34

तदेतत्सत्यं यथा सुदीप्तात्पाव कादु विस्फुलिङ्गाः सहस्रशः प्रभवन्ते सरूपाः ।
तथा क्षराद्द्विविधाः सोम्य भावाः प्रजायन्ते तत्र चैवापियन्ति ।।2।।

This is the truth. As from a blazing fire, sparks being like unto fire issue forth by thousands, so various Jivas are produced from the indestructible (Brahman), O Beloved youth, and also they return to Him.

–Mundaka 2-1-1

As a spider moves along the thread (it produces) and as from a fire tiny sparks fly in all directions, so from this Self emanate all organs, all words, all gods and all beings. Its secret name (Upanishad) is 'the Truth of truth'. The vital force is truth, and it is the truth of that.

–Brihadāranyaka Upanishad 2-1-20

As one fire, after it has entered the world, though one, takes different forms according to whatever it burns, so does the eternal Ātmā of all living beings, though one, takes a form according to whatever He enters and is outside all forms.

–Kathopanishad 2-5-9

दिव्यो ह्यमूर्तः पुरुषः स बाह्याभ्यन्तरो ह्यजः ।
अप्राणो ह्यमनाः शुभ्रो ह्यक्षरात् परतः परः ।।2।।

He is very luminous, without form; he is both without and within; unborn, without prāna, without mind, pure and greater than the great, the indestructible one.

–Mundaka 2-1-2

The wise man, who knows the Ātmā as bodiless, seated firmly in perishable bodies, great and all-pervading, does never grieve.

–Kathopanishad 1-2-22

It (Ātmā) moves and It moves not. It is distant and It is near. It is within all this and It is also outside all this.

–Ishāvāsya Upanishad 1-5

पुरुष एवेदं विश्वं कर्म तपो ब्रह्म परामृतम् ।
एतद्यो वेद निहितं गुहायां सोऽविद्याग्रन्थिं विकिरतीह सोम्य ।।10।।

The Purusha alone is this entire universe, Karma (sacrifice) penance, Brahman, the highest immortal; he who knows this, hidden in the cave of the heart, breaks the knot of ignorance even here (on earth), O gentle youth!

–Mundaka 2-1-10

OM. The knower of Brahman attains the highest. Here is a verse uttering the fact: "Brahman is

Truth, Knowledge and Infinite. He who knows that Brahman as existing in the intellect, which is lodged in the supreme space in the heart, enjoys, in identification with the all-knowing Brahman, all desirable things simultaneously."

–Taittiriya Upanishad 2-1-1

Free from pride and delusion, with the evil of attachment conquered, ever dwelling in the Self, their desires being completely stilled, liberated from the pairs of opposite known as pleasure and pain, the undeluded reach that Goal Eternal.

–Bhagavad Gita 15-5

Brahman is without doubt endless, beyond reason and analogy, beyond all proofs and causeless, knowing which the wise one becomes free.

–Amritabindupanishad 9

हिरण्मये परे कोशे विरजं ब्रह्म निष्कलम् ।
तच्छुभ्रं ज्योतिषां ज्योतिस्तद्यदात्मविदो विदुः । ।7 । ।

In the innermost golden sheath there is Brahman without stains and without parts. That is pure, that is the light of lights. That is what the knowers of the Atma know.

–Mundaka 2-2-9

The Brahman is known well, when it is known as the witness of every state of consciousness because (by such knowledge) he attains immortality. By his Self he attains strength and by knowledge, immortality.

–Kenopanishad 2-4

When a man after receiving instructions from a teacher directly realises this effulgent Self, the

Lord of all that has been and will be, he no longer wishes to hide himself from it.

–**Brihadāranyaka Upanishad 4-4-15**

The light of all lights, He is said to be beyond darkness; knowledge, the knowable, the goal of knowledge, seated in the hearts of all.

–**Bhagavad Gitā 13-17**

That alone is Brahman, without component parts, without doubt, and without taint. Realising "I am that Brahman" one becomes the immutable Brahman.

–**Amritabindupanishad 8**

न तत्र सूर्यो भाति न चन्द्रतारकं नेमा विद्युतो भान्ति कुतोऽयमग्निः ।
तमेव भान्तमनुभाति सर्वं तस्य भासा सर्वमिदं विभाति ।।20।।

The sun does not shine there, nor do the moon and the stars, nor these lightnings and much less this fire. When He shines, everything shines after Him. By His light all this is illumined.

–**Mundaka 2-2-10**

There the sun does not shine, neither do the moon and the stars; nor do these flashes of lightning shine. How can this fire shine? By His shining, all these shine; through His lustre all these are variously illumined.

–**Shvetāsvatara Upanishad 6-14**

That the sun illumines not, nor the moon, nor fire; that is My supreme abode, going whither they return not.

–**Bhagavad Gita 15-6**

ब्रह्मैवेदममृतं पुरस्ताद् ब्रह्म पश्चाद्ब्रह्म दक्षिणतश्चोत्तरेण ।
अधश्चोर्ध्वं च प्रसृतं ब्रह्मैवेदं विश्वमिदं वरिष्ठम् ।।22।।

That immortal Brahman is before, that Brahman is behind, to the right and to the left, below and above, all-pervading; Brahman alone is all this; it is the highest.

–Mundaka 2-2-11

This Ātmā is hidden in all beings and does not shine forth; but it is seen by subtle seers through their sharp and subtle intellect.

–Kathopanishad 1-3-12

As Hamsa (sun) He dwells in heaven; as Vasu He dwells in the sky; as fire He dwells on the Earth; as a guest He dwells in a house; He dwells in men, in Gods, in Truth, in ether. He is born in the waters, He is born in the earth, He is born in the sacrifices, He is born on the mountains; He is true and great.

–Kathopanishad 2-5-2

With hands and feet everywhere, with eyes and hands and mouths everywhere, with ears everywhere – He exists enveloping all.

–Bhagavad Gitā 13-15

He shines illuminating all the directions, above, below and others, as does the sun. In this way that God, the effulgent and adorable one, rules alone over all those that stand as the sources.

–Shvetāsvatara Upanishad 5-4

I alone am taught in the various Vedas, I am the revealer of the Vedānta or Upanishads, and I am also the knower of the Vedas. For me there is neither merit nor demerit, I suffer no destruction; I have no birth, nor any self-identity with the body and the organs.

–Kaivalya Upanishad 22

द्वा सुपर्णा सयुजा सखाया समानं वृक्षं परिषस्वजाते ।
तयोरन्यः पिप्पलं स्वाद्वत्त्यनश्नन्नन्यो अभिचाकशीति ।।2।।

*Two birds, inseparable companions, dwell upon
one and the same tree. One of them eats the sweet
and bitter fruits, the other looks on without eating.*

–Mundaka 3-1-1

*The two who enjoy the fruits of their good works
being seated in the cavity of the seat of the
Supreme, the knower of Brahman, call them
shadow and light, as also the performers of the
fivefold fires and those who have propitiated three
times the Nachiketa fire.*

–Kathopanishad 1-3-1

*Two birds that are ever associated and have
similar names cling to the same tree. Of these two,
one eats the fruit of divergent tastes and the other
looks on without eating.*

–Shvetāsvatara Upanishad 4-6

बृहच्च तद्दिव्यमचिन्त्यरूपं सूक्ष्माच्च तत्सूक्ष्मतरं विभाति ।
दूरात् सुदूरे तदिहान्तिके च पश्यत्स्विहैव निहितं गुहायाम् ।।7।।

*That (true Brahman) shines forth, vast, divine,
inconceivable, subtler than the subtle. It is far
beyond what is far and yet near here and seen
fixed in the cave of the heart by the wise.*

–Mundaka 3-1-7

*The Ātmā subtler than the subtle, greater than
the great, is seated in the heart of each living
being. He who is free from desire, with his mind
and the senses composed, beholds the majesty of
the Self and becomes free from sorrow.*

–Kathopanishad 1-2-20

The Self that is subtler than the subtle and greater than the great is lodged in the heart of (every) creature. Through the grace of the Lord, one who sees that Self desireless, and sees Its glory as God, becomes sorrowless.

–Shvetāsvatara Upanishad 3-20

Without and within all beings; the unmoving and also the moving; because of His subtlety He is incomprehensible; He is far and near.

–Bhagavad Gītā 13-15

वेदान्तविज्ञानसुनिश्चितार्थाः सन्न्यासयोगाद् यतयः शुद्धसत्त्वाः
ते ब्रह्मलोकेषु परान्तकाले परामृताः परिमुच्यन्ति सर्वे ।।6।।

Having without doubt well ascertained the import of the knowledge of Vedanta and having purified their minds by the yoga of renunciation, all anchorites attain the world of Brahman and at the time of death become fully liberated.

–Mundaka 3-2-6

Higher than heaven, seated in the cave (buddhi) that shines, (which) the self-controlled attain – the self-controlled, who being of pure minds have well ascertained the Reality, by the knowledge of Vedanta, and through sannyāsa *or renunciation. In the sphere of Brahman, at the time of cosmic dissolution, they all get liberated from the highest (apparent) immortality of the manifested universe.*

–Kaivalya Upanishad 3

यथा नद्यः स्यन्दमानाः समुद्रेऽस्तं गच्छन्ति नामरूपे विहाय।
तथा विद्वान् नामरूपाद् विमुक्तः परात्परं पुरुषमुपैति दिव्यम् ।।8।।

Just as the flowing rivers disappear in the sea, losing their names and forms, so also a seer freed from name and form goes to the Divine person who is greater than the great.

–Mundaka 3-2-8

O Somya, those rivers belonging to the east run to the east, and those belonging to the west run to the west. Rising from the sea, they go back to it and become one with it. Just as when they reach the sea, they do not know their separate identities – 'I am this river,' or 'I am that river.'

–Chhandogya Upanishad 6-10-1

Just as these rivers flowing towards the sea, when they have reached the sea, disappear, their names and forms perish and all is called sea, so also these sixteen parts of the witness that go towards the Purusha *disappear, their names and forms are destroyed and all is called* Purusha *alone.*

–Prasnopanishad 6-5

स यो ह वै तत्परमं ब्रह्म वेद ब्रह्मैव भवति नास्याब्रह्मवित्कुले भवति ।
तरति शोकं तरति पाप्मानं गुहाग्रन्थिभ्यो विमुक्तोऽमृतो भवति । ।९ । ।

He who knows that highest Brahman becomes Brahman. In his line no one who does not know Brahman will be born. He overcomes grief, good and evil and, being freed from the fetters of the heart, becomes immortal.

–Mundaka 3-2-9

By knowing the Deity comes the snapping of all bondages; on the attenuation of the pain-bearing obstructions comes the eradication of birth and death. From meditation on Him there accrues, on all of the body, the full divine power. And he becomes absolute and self-fulfilled.

–Shvetāsvatara Upanishad 1-11

He shines illuminating all the directions, above, below and others, as does the sun. In this way, that God, the effulgent and adorable one, rules alone over all those that stand as the sources.

–Shvetāsvatara Upanishad 5-4

Hari Om!

❑❑❑

TOPIC – VI
The Minor Upanishads

Since we have been discussing the classifications of the Upanishads into minor and major, the question naturally arises – what is the basis of this categorisation? Though the word 'minor' makes it amply clear about the content and the size vis-à-vis the major, there are some more yardsticks to consider.

The minor Upanishads focus on some aspects of the major Upanishads in greater detail. At times, a topic does not exist at all in any of the Upanishads, being new and a genuine addition to philosophy. Brahman blesses all sentient and insentient objects, therefore, anything can be taken up to give the status of His manifestation and raise it to the height of Brahman in identification.

Thus, the minor Upanishad came to supplement the study, but the general rule of classification is that all the Upanishads (except those with the commentary of Ādi Shankarāchārya) are also known as minor Upanishads and have been taken up here for a brief discussion. The Upanishads discussed here have the *shānti pātha* of the respective Vedas.

Paramahamsopanishad

In Param hamsa Upanishad the teacher is
Brahma, the creator and the student is the well-
known *Devarishi Nārada*. The question is similar
to that asked by Arjuna to Lord Krishna, in the
second chapter, regarding the *nishtā* of a *jnāni*,
and his life-style, to be emulated by others.

This Upanishad talks about the characteristics
of a *paramahamsa*. It is said that the bird *hansa*,
a heavenly swan, has the special faculty to
separate water from milk. The word *parama*
denotes the superlative degree of character, the
faculty of discrimination and dispassion.

This Upanishad lists the activities of the relative
relationship in the common physical and mental
plane of existence and negates them for spiritual
ideals to be the quality and characteristics of a
paramahamsa yogi. The *paramahamsa* yogi is a
sādhaka, a *sannyāsi*, who observes very rigid
austerity and penance and has achieved control
over the mind and senses. He is fit for the
beatitude of the knowledge of the Self, the
identity with the Ātmā.

At the time of practising penance and austerity,
he continues to be ignorant and not a man of
knowledge of the Self yet, as for a man with
knowledge of the Self, there is no discipline or
austerity to be practised. If at all he does so in
the interest of others or to guide the masses, in
the language of the *Gitā* it is *loka sangraha*.

Having given up all thoughts of the world,
realising the eternal Brahman, he lives in 'That',
conscious that "I am Him". That knowledge alone
is his holy thread, the vow. Having identified

himself with the Infinite One, the distinction between the two is totally gone.

The Upanishad concludes that the realisation by this *sādhaka* that "I am Brahman who is the One Infinite-Knowledge-Bliss" helps him attain his goal. The *paramahamsa* is the *jivan mukta* while breathing and the *videha mukta* while the body breathes no more.

Ãtmopanishad

In Ãtmā Upanishad, the teacher is the famous *Brahma vidyā* achārya, rishi Angiras. The corollary of this Upanishad has been discussed in the *Brihadāranyaka Upanishad*, in the second chapter, third section. This is an example of gross to subtle, known as *shaka chandra nyāya*, for teaching the knowledge of Brahman – "the maxim of the bough and the moon". (The distant moon is said to be on the bough.)

The physical body and the subtle body have been brought to the level of truth and both together become *satyam*. The *satyam* Brahman, Ãtmā, has become as though the outer Ãtmā and again the subtle mind, the *Chidabhāsa*, inner Ãtmā, enters as though to activate the activities (*anupravesha shruti*) remaining itself as the substratum of the two, too, the ultimate truth. The essence of this is that Brahman is the truth of the truth (*satyasya satyam iti*).

The *Paramātmā* has no relation with the body, but for the sake of easy understanding by the beginner, here it is shown as the outer and the inner Ãtmā respectively. Thus, *satyam* is the name.

The narration is at three levels. The first level describes the gross body parts, the second part is the description of the subtle mind as experiencer and the third part is the attributeless Brahman. To understand the text, the catchword is *Purusha*, which does not stand for Ātmā – the normal meaning – but for the experience of the subtle mind in this Upanishad. Here, Brahman is both the *murta* and *amurta prapancha*. *Murta* is that which can be seen and *amurta* is that which cannot be seen. (The gross body can be seen, whereas the subtle body cannot be seen). This is at the individual level, as described in this Upanishad, which corresponds to the supernatural level; space and air are *amurta*, whereas fire, water and the earth are *murta prapancha*.

Thus, both at the micro and macro level it is identified with the derived *satyam* and the essence of this is the Supreme Lord. Concluding it, the teacher says: "He is all-pervading, unthinkable and indescribable. He is to be worshipped according to the precepts of the Vedas. He is the Supreme *Purusha*, who is called *Paramātmā*."

Gist: The essence of that which is gross, mortal, limited and defined is the eye, just as it is the solar orb with reference to Gods. All gross and subtle forms are Brahman. Therefore, the description of Brahman is given as 'not this, not that', because there is no other more appropriate description than this.

Its name is *satyasya satyam* – 'truth of the truth'. The vital force is the truth and it is the truth of truths.

Amritabindupanishad

Among the five Bindu Upanishads, this Upanishad occupies a very important place. *Brahmabindu* and *Amritabindu* are literally the same except for minor changes here and there. This Upanishad with 22 verses is packed with the idea of the means for liberation through inculcating control of the mind. The mind is called impure when it is loaded with desires. It is an ignorant mind that is the cause of bondage. A desireless mind is the means to liberation, the path to the Truth. The knowledge that 'I am the Witness-Consciousness' is liberation, which is absence of identification with the body and its relationship. To purify the mind, meditation on OM with attributes has been initially prescribed and later on with the attributeless, as OM stands for both.

The process of identification with Brahman has three tiers:

➤ Listening to the teacher – *shravanam*.

➤ The analysis, reflection on the teaching – *mananam*.

➤ Contemplation – *nididhyāsanam*.

Nishtā or the desire to be identified with Brahman has been prescribed to attain the goal – that is the ultimate truth. Verse number 8 is a *mahavākya* that says: "That alone is Brahman, without component parts, without doubt and without taint. Realising 'I am that Brahman' one becomes the immutable Brahman."

The Brahma *swarupam* has been described, which is helpful for contemplation and for owning up. The benefits of knowledge of the Self or liberation are described as freedom from the cycle of birth and death – the central point around which *sādhanā* revolves. Therefore, the name *amritabindu* is very apt, as it means drop of nectar. It has also been suggested that even the Scriptures are to be renounced after their aim of providing mental purity through rituals and meditation is achieved. The systematic teaching of knowledge of the Self by the Scriptures through *neti, neti* ('not this, not that'), the best way of identifying with Brahman, has also been implicitly made use of.

Tejabindupanishad

Teja Bindu Upanishad is the last of the five Bindu Upanishads of the *Atharva Veda*. This Upanishad presents the Supreme Ãtmā that dwells in the hearts, as the Self-effulgent and subtle one, realised through the highest order of meditation.

There are disciplines on initiation into disciplehood for purification of the mind and sense control, which have been given special names, such as *Anava, Shākta* and *Sambhava*. It is pointed out that the meditation prescribed is difficult and, therefore, lots of practice with determination is required, such as control of food, passion and desires. It says that he should be the one who makes the inaccessible accessible, whose sole aim is to serve the teacher and his own cause only as the *sādhaka*.

Next, the nature of the Ãtmā to be meditated upon is given here. It is devoid of form, unchangeable, unconditioned, uncontainable and without substratum, but the substratum of all. It is higher than the highest, unthinkable and free from the experiences of the waking state.

Then the Upanishad speaks about the obstacles and disqualifications on the path to realisation, such as merely having an academic interest, being perturbed by the pairs of opposites etc, and all these are known as the *āsuri sampat*. Persever-ance, fitness of the body and the purity of mind is required – conduct that is conducive to the knowledge of the Self. The Upanishad concludes that in he who is free from these obstacles, the Supreme Brahman becomes manifest, as his highest refuge is Brahman.

Sarvasāra Upanishad – *Atharva Veda*

This Upanishad is the concentrated wisdom of Vedānta in the form of questions and answers on the terms and terminologies used, to understand and practise the study of the Upanishads. The fundamental nature of twenty-three topics has been explained here. These include bondage, liberation and ideals for the seeker of the Truth, the identity of the *Jivātmā* with *Paramātmā*, definition of *Māyā* and Brahman, the *Jivan mukta*, the essence of Truth and knowledge and the definition of esoteric and philosophic terms.

This Upanishad is very useful in our pursuit of Vedāntic philosophy. Questions and answers are to the point and elaborated wherever necessary, much like an encyclopaedia, for proper understanding of what is what in Vedānta text (*mimāmsā*) to identify the self as *aham brahmāsmi*.

These questions and answers are given below:

What is bondage (*bandha*) of the soul?

The Self falsely taking upon the body and identifying with it is bondage.

What is liberation (*moksha*)?

The freedom from identification with the body and body-related objects is liberation.

What is nescience (*avidyā*)?

That which causes this wrong identification is nescience.

What is knowledge (*vidyā*)?

That which removes the mistaken notion is knowledge, i.e., freedom from ignorance.

What are (meant by) the states of waking (*jāgrat*), the dreaming (*swapna*), the dreamless sleep (*sushupti*) and the fourth state (*turiya*)?

Jāgrat is that state during which the *Jivātmā* enjoys the gross objects of the senses such as sight, sound, taste etc, through the fourteen organs, including the mind.

Swapna is that state during which the *Jivātmā* experiences things through the subtle organs associated with the *vāsanās*, divested of desires.

The *Jivātmā* experiences the dreamless state without any special enjoyment of consciousness on account of the absence of the active sense organs.

Turiya is that state during which the *Jivātmā* is a mere witness to the existence of the previous three states, though it is in itself without existence or non-existence and during which it is one uninterrupted Consciousness.

What are the five sheaths (*koshas*)?

Annamaya sheath is the aggregate of the material formed by food, maintained by food and lost to food. When the vital air (*prāna*) flows through *annamaya* sheath, it is *Prānamaya* sheath or subtle energy. When the Ātmā connected to the above two sheaths performs the functions of the sense organs it is called *Manomaya* sheath. When the Ātmā shines, being united with these three sheaths and cognisant of the differences and non-differences thereof, it is called *Vijnānamaya* sheath. When the four sheaths remain in their own cause, which is Knowledge (Brahman), in the same way as the latent banyan tree remains in the banyan seed, then it is known as *Ānandamaya kosha.*

What is meant by the doer (*kartā*), *Jiva*, the five groups (*Panchavarga*), *Kshetrajna*, the witness (*Sākshi*), *Kutastha* and *Antaryāmi*?

Kartā is the one who possesses the body and the internal organs through their respective desires proceeding from the idea of pleasure and pain. *Jiva* is the deluded one which thinks that this body, obtained through the effects of good and bad deeds, is its own, not so obtained.

The five groups are – (1) *Mānas*: *mānas, buddhi, ahanakāra* (creating uncertainty, certitude, flitting thought and egoism); (2) *Prāna*: *prāna, apāna, vyāna, samāna* and *udāna*; (3) *Sattva, rājas* and *tamas*; (4) The five elements: earth, water, fire, air and space; (5) *Dharma* and its opposite, *Adharma*.

Consciousness that manifests itself therein is called *Kshetrajna* – the knower of the *kshetra*, the body.

The witness (*sākshi*) is that conscious one that is aware of the appearance and disappearance (of the three states) of the knower, known and the knowledge, who is himself not affected by this appearance and disappearance and who is Self-effulgent.

Kutastha is he who is found without exception in the *Buddhi* (mind) of all creatures from Brahman down to ants and who is shining as Ātmā and dwells as witness to the *buddhi* of all creatures.

Antaryāmi is the Ātmā that shines as the ordainer, being within all bodies like the thread on which beads are strung and serving to know the cause of the several differences of *Kutastha* and others associated with him.

Who is *Pratyāgātmā*?

He is of the nature of truth, wisdom, eternity and bliss. He has no vehicles of the body. He is abstract wisdom itself, like a mass of pure gold that is devoid of the changes or forms of the ornaments. He is of the nature of mere consciousness. He is that which shines as *Chaitanya* and Brahman and is the meaning of the word *tvam*.

Who is *Paramātmā*?

It is He who is associated with truth, wisdom, eternity, bliss, omniscience etc, who is subject to the vehicle of *Māyā* and who is the meaning of the word *Tat* (that) in *Tattwamasi*.

What is Brahman?

Brahman is that which is free from all vehicles, which is Absolute Consciousness devoid of particularities, which is *Sat*, which is without a second, which is bliss. It is the pure, the noumenal, the true and the indestructible, the *Sat-Chit-Ānanda*.

What is *satya*?

It is the *Sat* (the state of being), which is the aim pointed out by the Vedas. It is not affected by the three periods of time. It is that which continues to exist during the three periods of times. It is one without a second. It is that which does not perish even though space, time, matter and cause perish – pure existence.

What is *ananta*?

It is that which is without destruction. It is not subject to the six modifications like birth, growth, death etc.

What is bliss (*ānanda*)?

It is the seat of all sentient beings like the ocean of water; it is eternal, pure, part-less, and non-dual – an attribute of the attributeless.

Of how many kinds are substances?

There are three kinds: *Sat*, *Asat* and *mithyā* (illusion). *Sat* alone is Brahman. *Asat* is that which is not. *Mithyā* is the illusory ascription to Brahman of the universe that is not, though it is experienced.

What is *Māyā*?

She is matter and has no independent existence. She appears in Brahman like clouds in the sky. She has no beginning, but ends on *ātyāntika pralayam*. Her seat is indescribable. She has varieties of differences as extolled by the wise. She appears as *mula prakriti* and *guna-sāmya* (a state where the three *gunas* – *satva*, *rājas* and *tamas* – are found in equilibrium), *avidyā*, and other forms, transforming herself into the form of the universe – like a projection in a dream. *Āvarana* and *Vikshepa sakti* are its two functions.

Brahmopanishad – *Atharva Veda*

Brahman Upanishad is intended to give a clear idea of the nature of Ātmā. The Ātmā has four states of consciousness (*avasthā*), four seats and four places of meditation for better appreciation of *nirguna dhyāna*. Here the teacher is Pippalāda and the student is Shaunaka, a great ritualist and householder. The four seats are the navel, the heart, the throat and the head. The four states of consciousness are the waking state, sleep, dreamless sleep and the transcendental state. In these four states He is Brahmā, Vishnu, Rudra and the Supreme Indestructible One respectively. The heart is the abode of the *Devas*, *prāna*, Supreme *prāna* and light, as also the Immanent Cause and the *Mahat* principle.

Here *prāna* has been glorified as the glory of the Ātmā, the life of the *Devas*, i.e., the *Indriyas*. The *Purusha* residing in the heart, the city of Brahman, has been glorified with all attributes, attributed to the attributeless Brahman, such as all-pervading, Self-effulgent and so on. The twice born (three *varnas*) have been stated to be the blessed ones for being able and entitled to perform the daily rituals which have far-reaching effects in purifying the mind, thus leading to the threshold of the knowledge of the Self.

Many analogies have been given to the process for the knowledge of the Self, such as kindling the fire through '*arni* wood' rubbing, churning

113

butter from the curd and the like. The secret and sacred Ātmā has to be discovered as the very Self. This Ātmā is neither perceivable, nor be imagined, nor searched, for all attempts to know the Ātmā are fruitless, as it is the very searcher. The Self is the very essence of everything.

Āruni Upanishad – Sāma Veda

This is an Upanishad in which Lord Brahmā is the teacher and Āruni, son of Aruna, is the student, the sādhaka. Here the topic is the characteristic of a sannyāsi in search of realisation, which is exactly like Paramahamsa Upanishad, discussed earlier. Āruni enquires from Brahmā, the creator, about the way one can relinquish work altogether.

In reply, Brahmā enumerates a list of activities to be renounced, e.g., attachment and vaidika karmas, to achieve the status of a sannyāsi. One has to renounce even the Gāyatri mantra and the holy thread, meditating only on OM. In order to meet the requirements of the body and breath together, one has to resort to alms (bhikshā) with a small loincloth, just sufficient to cover the body so that one can enter a village to beg, while adhering to societal norms of decency.

Having given up all physical belongings, one should give up the ego also to discover the Truth "I am that Sat-Chid-Ānanda Brahman". These are the instructions of the guru to initiate the student into the fold of knowledge of the Self, a seeker, and a sannyāsi.

Kaivalya Upanishad – *Atharva Veda*

Kaivalya Upanishad is a highly philosophical and concise one among the minor Upanishads. The student is the famous rishi Ashwalāyana of the *Rig Veda* and the teacher is none other than the creator, Brahmā. After prostrating before the teacher in the proper manner, the student requests that he be taught the knowledge of the Self. He also glorifies the knowledge to show why he seeks it.

In reply, Brahmā says that one should practise faith, devotion and meditation. These three words indicate listening (*sravanam*), reflection (*mananam*) and contemplation (*nididhyā-sanam*).

In this Upanishad, the last topic of contemplation (*nididhyāsanam*) has been taken up first. All the preparations regarding the seat, posture and invocation of the grace of the teacher and Lord have been taught as in the sixth chapter of the *Bhagavad Gītā*. Here again, knowledge is compared to the fire, obtained from rubbing '*arni* wood', where the mind is the lower *arni* and OM is the upper *arni* and the fire of knowledge is capable of burning the fuel, the ignorance, leading to liberation.

The benefit of this knowledge of the Self has been given as *jivan mukti* while living and *videha mukti* after the fall of the body. It is the law of nature that one becomes that on which one meditates upon. In this context, the *swarupa* of the Self is that it is eternal, without cause and effect, as well as a witness of all. It means that it is beyond the *dharma* of the body, not affected by it, which is the nature of the Ātmā.

115

Having understood these facts and accepted the glory of the Ātmā, one discovers himself as the very Ātmā. There is no question of *becoming*. It *is*, it *was* and it will *be so* all the time. Some more qualities of Brahman are given – it is manifest in the cave of the heart, part-less, undivided, division-less, witness of everything but unattached. One who meditates upon this Brahman shall discover that the liberated one is in the state of *Kaivalyam*, one with the Infinite as the very name of the Upanishad suggests.

For some students who may not be up to the desired level of the purity of the mind to be blessed by the knowledge, *Rudra jāpam* has been prescribed as *sādhanā*. *Rudra upāsanā* will remove impurities of the mind and also destroy the effects of bad actions (*pāpa*). *Kaivalya Upanishad* has many *mahāvākyas*, which other Upanishads do not have, generally. Though small, it is a beautiful and complete Upanishad.

After gaining knowledge of the Self, the statements of the student that he is the teacher, the Scripture, the subject matter of the Scripture etc are a beautiful illustration of the advaita vision. This is similar to the verse in the *Bhagavad Gitā*, Chapter 4: *'Brahma'rpanam brahma havir, brahmagnau brahmana hutam.'* Verse 15 depicts the creation of fire and other constituents of the universe, *'adhyāropa apavāda nyāya'*. This is one of the methods to impart knowledge of Brahman saying *"not this, not that"*.

Shvetāsvatara Upanishad – *Krishna Yajurveda*

Doubts have surfaced whether the commentary of Ādi Shankarāchārya is there for this

Upanishad also, as the eleventh Upanishad. A close study of the language and style, though, does not confirm the claim. But it is a very good Upanishad and many of its verses are found in the *Bhagavad Gitā* and in contemporary Upanishads.

All-pervasive Brahman is eulogised in the form of a wheel. It says: *"They saw Him as having one rim, three tiers, sixteen ends and fifty spokes, twenty fasteners, six sets of eight, one bondage of numerous forms, three different paths and a single delusion that is the cause of the two."*

He alone rules all the sources as one rim is the support. The three tiers are indicated by the three *gunas* of *satva*, *rajas* and *tamas*, which are the constituents of nature. The sixteen ends indicate the elements of earth, water, fire, air, and space and the eleven organs (mind, the five sense organs, and the five organs of action) for its ends, the manifestation. The fifty spokes indicate fifty different notions like disabilities and satisfaction, five different misconceptions, which are delusion, obscurity, extreme delusion, gloom, and utter darkness.

The disabilities are twenty-eight in number. Satisfaction is of nine kinds and success is of eight kinds. The twenty fasteners are ten organs and their objects, like sound, form etc. The six sets of eight indicate that nature has eight folds i.e. earth, water, fire, air, space, mind, intellect and egoism. The eight body substances are external-internal, skin, flesh, blood, fat, bone, marrow and semen. The eight states of mind are virtue, knowledge, detachment, majesty, vice, ignorance, attachment and poverty. The eight supernatural beings are Brahma, Prajāpati, the Gods, Gandharvas, *Yakshas*, demons, manes (spirits of the dead) and ghosts. The eight qualities of mind are kindness to all beings, tolerance, absence of jealousy, purity, ease, goodness, generosity and contentment. Bondage is a variety of desires such as heaven, a son, food etc. The three different paths are righteousness, unright-eousness and knowledge. A single delusion is identification with the body, sense, mind, intellect, caste etc. The cause of two is virtues and vice.

After elaborately discussing the eternal Brahman, knowledge of the Self, perception and approach, the Upanishad also clarifies a point of lurking doubt about alternate means to liberation. The Upanishad says: "It is possible on one condition that if one can fold the sky like leather, there shall be an end to sorrow without knowing the Effulgent One."

Nārāyana Upanishad – *Krishna Yajurveda*

Nārāyana Upanishad enumerates the creation of *prāna* (*pancha prāna*), *mānas* (*antahkarana*), body-mind complex, the five great elements, the *devatas* like Indra, *Kāla* (time concept) and the Vedas by Lord Nārāyana Himself. The creator is addressed by several names such as Brahmā, Vishnu, Shiva, which are functional names of one and the same eternal God. This explains the cause and effect relationship. The cause is always present in the effect, before, after and during its existence as a substratum.

This Upanishad makes a reference to the eight-lettered sacred name, which is the name of the Lord. The OM is a single syllable. *Namo* is a double-syllable word and *Nārāyanāya* contains five syllables. This came to be known as the *Ashtākshara* of Lord Nārāyana and is specified for *upāsanā* and *jāpa* (recitation), which has the potency for purification of the mind and thus makes one eligible for the yoga of knowledge.

The mantra *Aum Namo Nārāyanaya* is the destroyer of the five great sins – the sin of stealing gold, drinking alcohol, the murder of a Brahmin, unlawful association with the wife of a guru and the burning of a house. The efficacy of this mantra is that all sins committed before reciting the mantra get absolved.

The Upanishad glorifies the name of Nārāyana, who is the abode of all bliss and the destroyer of all committed sins. Nārāyana is the creator, sustainer and resolver of all the gross and subtle bodies and also the very essence of all, who is beyond time, space and qualities.

Vajrasuchi Upanishad – *Sāma Veda*

We have all heard of the Vajrāuda of Indra, which is a most powerful weapon that destroyed the *asuras* and was made out of the bones offered by the great, selfless rishi Dadhichi – a shining example of sacrifice for protecting *dharma* against *adharma*. The same essence is used here for knowledge, the destroyer of ignorance (the *asuras*).

The Vedas dwell on the divisions of relative activities into four groups depending on one's expertise in different professions, known by their *gunas*, such as Brāhmana, Kshatriya, Vaishya and Shudra. The job descriptions were learning/ teaching, the warrior class meant to protect the community, business/commerce and manual labourers. This division was based upon practical considerations, meant for better performance only and not a point for debate but a free premise for an ideal, homogenous and prosperous society. This Upanishad defines what Brāhmin – the superior one – means. The superiority is the content of Self-realisation that applies to one and all. In this Upanishad, it is said to be the cause (creator) of the other three *varnas*. The Brāhmin is first to appear in the creation of beings and in no way more important in comparison to the other *varnas*, in consideration of the Jiva, body, class, birth, karma or *jñāna*, as these are seen in other persons too, other than the Brāhmin.

Again, the Upanishad concludes that the Brāhmin does not mean anything that has been considered before, but Brāhmin means a person of knowledge of the Self, whosoever s/he may be, by class or caste, as all other considerations do not have any bearing. The purity of conduct is to be free from malice, emotion, thirst for worldly objects, desires and delusion. The mind is free from pride and egoism and it is declared by the Vedas, the *Purānas* and historical texts that a person who possesses these qualities is a Brāhmin. Brāhmin means a *guna* Brāhmin and not one by birth (*janama*).

Muktikopanishad – *Shukla Yajurveda*

This Upanishad is a dialogue between Lord Rāma and the devotee, Lord Hanumān. This Upanishad reveals the Vedas, its branches, the number of Upanishads therein and also the effective number of Upanishads in vogue.

The main question here is the means for salvation and Lord Rāma prescribes the repetition of His name and salvation is defined as *Salokya* (His abode) and one attains His *swarupa* (being) by leaving the mortal in Kāshi when Lord Shiva initiates him. Lord Rāma mentions the names of 108 Upanishads and the essence of them. Study of the Upanishads through a competent teacher will destroy sins. In the present example, Lord Rāma Himself is the teacher and Lord Hanumān is the student.

This Upanishad shows the way on how to get a teacher and also indicates the fitness of the student who has purity of mind. The means to attain purity of mind are described as spiritual practice of karma, *satsanga*, *prāṇāyāma* and *upāsanā* etc. As a force to control the mind, suppression is not recommended, but discrimination (*viveka*) alone will help see things as they are, i.e., the understanding of limitations and completeness etc.

Emphasis has been placed to watch over *vāsanā*, and restraint of the mind (*mānas*), which will be fruitful. If practised for a long time, one will attain purity of mind. Lord Rāma shows His real *swarupa* as the *nirguna Brahman* by explaining what the attributes of the attributeless Brahman are – the eternal, destroyer of *samsāra*, non-dual, supreme, and not affected by any object or quality.

After glorifying the nature of the formless Brahmān, Lord Rāma extols His disciple Hanumān to recognise these attributes (contemplation) as 'I am that birthless, the shining one, all-pervading, pure' etc, and says that this is the divine knowledge of Brahman.

Ātmabodha Upanishad – *Rig Veda*

Ātma Bodha Upanishad deals first with the *saguna upāsanā* of Brahman with attributes. Lord Krishna is saluted in the form of Vishnu, with four hands, holding the conch, mace, disc and club. The Upanishad describes the name, form and virtues of the Lord in various ways, given in our Scriptures for meditation and also the sacred mantra *Aum Namo Nārāyanāya*, which is the remover of sins of various types and degrees. It helps in attaining purity of mind and firmness, too. This is also the means to attain heaven, which is His abode and the liberation that comes in stages.

The *Pranava AUM* is also the name of the Lord with attributes and without attributes. *AUM* is split into three letters, A, U, M, which indicate the three states of the existence of the *saguna Brahman* and the fourth state, *turiya*, is the silence between the chant of one syllable and another, the *nirguna Brahman* (*Māndukya Upanishad*). The Upanishad says that devotion and *upāsanā* towards the Lord is the gain of *prajnāna*, the special wisdom to look upon one's self as in all, as I am Ātmā, limitless, bliss, without any attachment and desires, I am the *Jiva* as well as *Deva*. The student owns everything in the universe himself (The Upanishad gives a list of such perceptions).

While owning up the spirit, all matters stand rejected as not being owned and so also that which indicates the duality between the Jiva and Ātmā (Brahman). *Avidyā sutra* of *Brihadāranyaka Upanishad* is reflected here as the fruit of seeing duality, i.e., going from birth to birth. Criticism has been showered on the ignorant one (*ajnāni*) who identifies oneself with the body, mind and body-related relations, as the Chārvākas do. This is a beautiful description in detail, identifying the various attributes of the attributelessness and the Self as Ātmā, the essence of both *nirguna* and *saguna*

Hari Om Tat Sat!

Hari Om!

❑❑❑

TOPIC - VII
Upanishads in Vogue

NO.	NAME OF UPANISHAD	VEDA	NO.	NAME OF UPANISHAD	VEDA
1.	ADHYÃTMA	SY	21.	(BRIHAT) JABÃLÃ	A
2.	ADVAIYA TARAKA	SY	22.	BRAHMA	KY
3.	AITAREYA	R	23.	(BRAHMA) VIDYA	KY
4.	AKSHAMALIKA	R	24.	CHHÃNDOGYA	S
5.	AKSHI	KY	25.	DEVI	A
6.	(AMRITA) BINDU	KY	26.	DAKSHINÃ (MURTY)	KY
7.	(AMRITA) NÃDA	KY	27.	DARS ANA	S
8.	(ANNA) PURNÃ	A	28.	DATTÃTREYA	A
9.	ÃRUNI	S	29.	DHYÃNA (BINDU)	KY
10.	(ATHARVA) SIRA	A	30.	EKÃKSHARA	KY
11.	(ATHARVA) SHIKA	A	31.	GANAPATI	A
12.	ÃTMÃ	A	32.	GARBHA	KY
13.	ÃTMA BHODHA	R	33.	GARUDA	A
14.	AVADHUTA	KY	34.	GOPÃLA TAPANI	A
15.	AVYAKTA	S	35.	HAMSA	SY
16.	BAHVRICHA	R	36.	HAYAGRIVA	A
17.	BHÃVANÃ	A	37.	ISHÃVASYA	SY
18.	BHASMA (JABÃLÃ)	A	38.	JABÃLÃ	SY
19.	BHIKSHU	SY	39.	JABÃLÃ DARSHAN	S
20.	BRIHADÃRANYAKA	SY	40.	JABÃLI	S

NO.	NAME OF UPANISHAD	VEDA	NO.	NAME OF UPANISHAD	VEDA
41.	KAUSHITAKI	R	70.	PARABRAHMA	A
42.	KAIVALYA	KY	71.	(PARAMA) HAMSA	SY
43.	KALAGNIRUDRA	KY	72.	(PARAMAHAMSA) PARIVRAJAKA	A
44.	KALI (SANTARANA)	KY	73.	PASUPATA	A
45.	KARA	KY	74.	(PRĀNA) AGNIHOTRA	KY
46.	KATHA	KY	75.	PRASNA	A
47.	KENA	S	76.	(RĀMA) RAHASYA	A
48.	KRISHNA	A	77.	(RĀMA) TAPANI	A
49.	KSHURIKA	KY	78.	(RUDURA) HRIDAYA	KY
50.	KUNDIKA	S	79.	RUDRĀKSHAJABĀLĀ	S
51.	MAHĀNĀRĀYANA	A	80.	SARASWATI RAHASYA	KY
52.	MAHATSANYĀSA	S			
53.	MAHAVĀKYA	A	81.	SARVASĀRA	KY
54.	MANDALĀBRAHMANA	SY	82.	SĀVITRI	S
55.	MĀNDUKYA	A	83.	SHĀNDILYA	A
56.	MAITRAYĀNI	S	84.	SARABHA	A
57.	MAITREYI	S	85.	SHARIRAKA	KY
58.	MANTRIKĀ	SY	86.	SATYAYANI	SY
59.	MUKTIKA	SY	87.	SKANDA	KY
60.	MUDGALA	R	88.	SUKARAHASYA	KY
61.	MUNDAKA	A	89.	SITĀ	A
62.	NĀDA (BINDU)	R	90.	SUBĀLĀ	SY
63.	NĀRADA PARIVRAJAKA	A	91.	SOUBHAGYALAKSHMI	R
			92.	SHVETĀSVATARA	KY
64.	NĀRĀYANA	KY	93.	SURYA	A
65.	NIRALAMBA	SY	94.	TĀRĀSĀRA	SY
66.	NIRVĀNA	R	95.	TAITTIRIYA	KY
67.	(NARSIMHA) TAPANI	A	96.	TEJO (BINDU)	KY
68.	PAINGALA	SY	97.	TRIPURA	R
69.	PANCHABRAHMA	KY	98.	TRIPURATAPANI	A

NO.	NAME OF UPANISHAD	VEDA	NO.	NAME OF UPANISHAD	VEDA
99.	TRISIKHIBRAHMANA	SY	104.	YĀJNAVALKYA	SY
100.	TURIYATITA	SY	105.	(YOGA) C UDĀ (MANI)	S
101.	VAJRASUCHIKA	S	106.	(YOGA) KUNDALINI	KY
102.	VĀRĀHA	KY	107.	(YOGA) SIKHĀ	KY
103.	VASUDEVA	S	108.	YOGA TATVA	KY

R - RIG VEDA

S - SĀMA VEDA

SY - SHUKLA YAJURVEDA

KY - KRISHNA YAJURVEDA

A - ATHARVA VEDA

Note:

➤ The study of the Upanishads is not to be pursued independently but only with the help of a qualified teacher, if the study is to be blessed.

➤ Knowledge of the Self is not to be mistaken for self-study.

➤ Enquiry of the Self means enquiry into Scriptural teachings such as "Who am I?" It takes recourse to the analysis of Vedāntic statements so that the understanding is free from doubts and misunderstandings.

➤ Vedānta uses the particular word to indicate different meanings in different contexts. For example, the word 'Brahman' has different meanings at different points or context and the dictionary meaning will not suffice on all occasions and only lead to confusion. Vedic usage of words and sentences is not subject to punctuation.

➤ To study Vedic Scriptures, the primary meaning is first taken. If that contradicts the context, then from the previous/ subsequent verses the correct meaning has to be inferred.

Hari Om!

❏❏❏

Bibliography

Principal Upanishads – Part I
by Swami Shivānanda

Chhāndogya Upanishad
by Swami Lokeswarananda

Brihadāranyaka Upanishad
by Swami Madhavanada

Svetāsvatara Upanishad
by Swami Gambhrananda

Minor Upanishads
by Swami Madhavananda

The Bhagavad Gitā
by Swami Chidbhavananda

Thirty Minor Upanishads
by K. Narayanasvami Aiyar

Glossary

Anātma:
Gross body made up of matter.

Dhaharakasa:
Symbolic space in the heart for meditation.

Garuda:
A swift bird, symbolic vehicle of Lord Vishnu.

Guru Paramparā:
The lineage of teachers of Vedānta.

Hiranyagarbha:
Consciousness limited by the *upādhi* (title) of aggregate subtle bodies.

Homa kunda:
Place prepared for sacrificial fire in which oblations are offered.

Ishwara:
Pure Consciousness combined with Māyā.

Jivātmā:
Consciousness obtained in the individual body.

Karma:
Action in general, ritualistic worship.

Mithyā jagat:
Unreal world. Though we experience this, it does not have independent existence.

Nirguna Brahma sādhanā:
Meditation on attributeless Brahman.

Pāpam:
Result of actions not approved by the Scriptures.

Paramātmā:
Pure Consciousness at the macro level.

Punyam:
Result of noble actions known as merit.

Saguna Brahma upāsanā:
Meditation on Brahman with attributes.

Samanvaya adhikaranam:
'Consistency' as the proof of central theme.

Sannyāsa:
Renunciation of home and hearth.

Sirovrata:
A vow in which fire is carried on the head.

Swarga:
Heaven.

Swarupa lakshanam:
Inherent attributes.

Tatastha lakshanam:
Indirect (casual) attributes.

Varuna:
God of rains.

Vibhuti:
Divine glories.

Virāt:
Consciousness limited or conditioned by the *upadhi* of aggregate of gross bodies.

HINDOOLOGY BOOKS

Rs. 150/-
4186 D • pp: 260 • Size: 7.25" x 9.5"

Rs. 150/-
9524 D • pp: 240 • Size: 7.25" x 9.5"

Rs. 140/-
9408 D • pp: 208 • Size: 7.25" x 9.5"

Rs. 499/- • Colour (H.B.)
9983 D • pp: 174 • Size: 8.5" x 11"

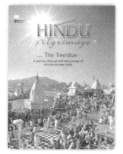

Rs. 499/- • Colour (H.B.)
4154 A • pp: 186 • Size: 8.5" x 11"

Rs. 120/-
4187 E • pp: 144 • Size: 7.25" x 9.5"

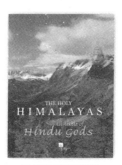

Rs. 399/- • Colour (H.B.)
9984 E • pp: 96 • Size: 8.5" x 11"

Rs. 150/- • Colour
9503 C • pp: 136 • Size: 7.25" x 9.5"

Rs. 399/- • Colour (H.B.)
4151 A • pp: 148 • Size: 8" x 10"

PUSTAK MAHAL®
Delhi • Mumbai • Patna • Hyderabad • Bengaluru

www.pustakmahal.com

HINDOOLOGY BOOKS

Rs. 160/- • 2 Colour (H.B.)
4125 B • pp: 248 • Size: 7.25" x 9.5"

Rs. 250/- • 2 Colour (H.B.)
4128 D • pp: 328 • Size: 7.25" x 9.5"

9520 D • Rs. 120/-

9525 A • Rs. 150/-

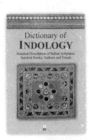

9516 D • Rs. 175/-

4183 A • Rs. 350/- (H.B.)

4179 A • Rs. 295/- (H.B.)

4184 B • Rs. 195/- (H.B.)

4177 C • Rs. 295/- (H.B.)

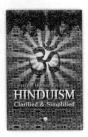

9506 B • Rs.249/- (HB)

9509 A • Rs.150/-

 PUSTAK MAHAL®
Delhi • Mumbai • Patna • Hyderabad • Bengaluru

www.pustakmahal.com

HINDOOLOGY BOOKS

9513 A • Rs.175/-

9510 B • Rs.120/-

9505 A • Rs.195/-

9514 B • Rs.60/-

9508 D • Rs.95/-

9507 C • Rs.96/-

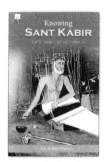

9504 D • Rs.96/-

4190 C • Rs. 160/-

9989 D • Rs. 96/-

PUSTAK MAHAL®
Delhi • Mumbai • Patna • Hyderabad • Bengaluru

www.pustakmahal.com

HINDOOLOGY BOOKS

4182 D • Rs. 96/-

9997 C • Rs. 80/-

4152 B • Rs. 96/-

4181 C • Rs. 195/-

9405 A • Rs. 195/-

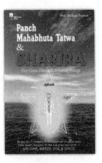

9407 C • Rs. 195/-

4131 C • Rs. 50/-

8284 D • Rs. 80/-

4124 A • Rs. 80/-

HINDOOLOGY BOOKS

9987 E • Rs. 150/-

4180 B• Rs. 96/-

4188 A • Rs. 160/-

4137 A • Rs. 80/-

9988 C • Rs. 60/-

4189 B • Rs. 80/-

4116 B • Rs. 80/-

4178 D • Rs. 80/-

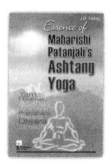

4133 A • Rs. 60/-